Emotional Maturity Series

The Language
of the
HEART

The Path of Emotional Maturity

Volume I

Chuck Spezzano, Ph. D.

Edited by Eric & Celia Taylor.

Cover design by Guter Punkt, Munich
www.guter_punkt.de

Printed and bound in Great Britain by
CPI Group (UK) Ltd, Croydon, CR0 4YY

ISBN 978-1-907798-27-6

To my mother

No longer in her body
But always in my heart
From whom I learned
So much about emotional maturity.

Thanks, Mom...

And to my father,

Long gone from this plane,
But still a deep abiding part of me.
From whom I learned to give
With my whole heart,

Thanks, Dad...

Acknowledgments

Yo, Team! Good Work!

We've done it again.

*To Napua, and Charlie in the office
who keeps us humming;*

To Robyn who keeps the land flourishing;

To Harryine for personal support;

To Chris for technical support;

To Sunny for great help in ordering the manuscript;

*To Eric and Celia for removing the flaws
and making it a better read;*

*To Lency, Chris and J'aime for fun,
inspiration and unflagging faith;*

*To A Course in Miracles for never
failing to teach and inspire!*

Thank you all.

Contents

Introduction

When I first began to write this book, I realized that it had been cooking in me for years. At first, I saw emotional maturity as an issue among a hundred other worthy issues to write about. But then I began to see that most of the issues that came up in coachings and workshops dealt to some degree with emotional immaturity. Emotional maturity was an issue that ran the gamut from beginners to my most advanced students. More and more I began to see the number of problems that were caused by lack of emotional maturity. I began to realize that the path of emotional maturity was actually a path to Oneness. Like all paths there were lessons and challenges, but emotional maturity as a path was viable, not only as a path of the heart, but as an expansion of the heart itself. When immaturity is removed, peace and love take place. Sometimes a bigger emotional conflict surfaces immediately once an old conflict is healed, because the deeper conflict was using the original conflict as a defense to hide itself. Yet, though things might seem to get worse when the deeper issue surfaced, if you took time to notice, you would recognize that you have moved forward in confidence and peace after each healing. If you had not healed, you would not have the wherewithal to deal with the deeper issue or let it come to the surface.

To the same extent that we are emotionally mature, we will be successful in relationships. This makes emotional maturity the quickest path to be even happier and thus the quickest path of spiritual growth. Relationships are meant to be the stairway to Heaven; they are what bring us to the Golden Life. The more emotional maturity we have, the more available, bonded and creative we will be. One way to measure emotional maturity is by a person's happiness. Denial doesn't really count as emotional maturity because we are simply deceiving ourselves now with an untrue cheerfulness, but later, in some rude awakening, we will have to pay the price for hiding the issues and emotions we need to deal with.

Over the years, what began to quicken the worthy theme of emotional maturity into an inspiration for me to write about was that I began to notice emotional immaturity in certain situations with some of my trainers. These were folks who had over a hundred days of training, some of them many more. I began to notice a gap in their training, a missing link in their education and it had to do with emotional maturity. Everything worked fine until they got into some conflict, either within themselves or with another. Then their understanding of emotions and healing principles seemed to fly out the window. I had the same reaction after seeing the first five TV shows of *In Treatment*, about a therapist, his clients and his process with his own supervisor/therapist. It was hard to believe the therapist's lack of awareness in regard to his own process and what he lacked in understanding about what was going on in himself.

In spite of my desire to educate my trainers about emotional maturity, I could also see that when the next level of pain came up they were just as lost and just as reactive as anyone else. I knew that more was needed and I knew that it was my responsibility to do something about it. Teaching about it at the beginning of every workshop did not seem to have much effect when issues came up. In a conflict, everyone's maturity and emotional intelligence seemed to regress greatly. I thought the best way to address this need was to write a book specifically addressing the principles of emotional maturity and then making it required reading for the Psychology of Vision Trainers.

Don't get me wrong, when issues come up for me, as they do for everyone, I get reactive also. The difference is, knowing that I'm off base, I soon 'bust myself'. I know that I'm dealing with old baggage and set off in a healing direction. I have minimized the time for my 'righteous reactions' and realize sooner rather than later what is up for my healing. I'm then quick to apologize for fighting and polluting the scene. Or I may not even reach the point of airing the upset out loud, but instead heal myself immediately so that I'm at peace and working proactively to make the situation better through forgiveness, self-forgiveness, commitment, gratitude, etc.

Heaven on Earth – the Path of Emotional Maturity reflects what I have learned over the years. I have found that if people do not learn and commit to these principles, they tend to use their emotions as weapons. And of course, if we do that, we won't escape turning these weapons on ourselves. We will experience the effect that we wished on others. We will torture ourselves as much as we torture and attack others with our emotions. If we use our emotions to attack or control, we won't be a very good partner and our partnership will tend to be all about us misusing others to take care of our own needs. This has little to do with relatedness and more to do with taking from others to meet our needs, which will keep us locked in a painful pattern of defeat and self-defeat.

When I was a boy and watched my parents fight, I had little understanding of what was going on. Emotions always seemed to be a very big deal, and dealing with them an even bigger deal. When I was 21 years of age, my uncle began doing astrology charts and volunteered to do one for me. When he finished, he found that I had strong fire (charisma), air (intelligence) and earth signs (dependability, solidity), but no water signs (feelings).

I said to my uncle, "How can that be possible? It seems to me that I have a lot of feelings. Maybe too many." My uncle gave a smile, half comic, half rueful and said, "What it means is that you have no natural control over your emotions."

I said, "Now that makes sense!"

That conversation took place over 40 years ago and I thought of it when I first began to be inspired to write this book. It seemed that someone who had no natural understanding or control over emotions, but who had to learn all the lessons from scratch, would be a good person to write such a book.

Learning about my emotions and emotional maturity was not easy for me. There were many hard fought lessons. But once I learned them, it made a big difference that added to the quality of my life and relationships.

What I can tell you after 40 years in the healing field is that this is one of the most crucial areas in life to learn if you wish for happiness and success. Let's face it, given the nature of life, we will all suffer, but we do not have to increase our suffering by foolish mistakes. We do not have to multiply our pain by blunders. By learning a number of principles and having the courage to live them, we can greatly decrease the number of emotional firebombs that explode in our lives. And if they do, we can minimize their effects by transformation and healing.

Emotional maturity will give us our heart back. With our heart, we will know our purpose, lead a balanced life in which we can enjoy our successes, and really know what love means. Without emotional maturity, we will get into frequent fights and painful melees. Or we live a life of boredom and deadness. We will take little responsibility for our lives and blame others when things don't go right. We will demand that life go our way and be terribly upset when it doesn't. We will demand that our relationships be all about us. We will fritter away creative and sexual energy to support getting our needs fulfilled, and will equate our needs being met with happiness. We will become an armored troop carrier for our ego in its desire to fight and make a lot of emotional baggage, which we will then expect others to deal with for us as if they were in the wrong. We will become a high-maintenance partner, making demands on everyone around us but with little ability to receive. We will move from indulgence to tantrum, not realizing how we are increasing our sacrifice and sense of being unrequited. It is easy enough to become blind and toxic, using our 'shtick' on others and ourselves.

If we follow the path of emotional maturity on the other hand, we give up our secret need for separation that occurs with each emotional attack and self-attack, and we finally find peace. We learn the joys of joining with others and so find the opening to transcendence. Life becomes an adventure, not a score about being on top or getting our way. We begin to find our way Home. We realize that our happiness is a team effort, gained not by what others do for us but by what we give to them. We find our life getting better by stages and we lead the way for others to follow. Instead of being a 'high-needs' and demanding person, we restore what was lost to us and to others. We shine and others become inspired by who we are. For some who are lost and in the darkness, we light the way back.

With emotional maturity, we learn that our happiness is in our hands and we stop being afraid of our greatness. We take what life gives us and use it as an opportunity to leap forward. At even deeper levels, we begin to take responsibility for what is occurring in our lives and start to dream a happier dream on our way to awakening altogether. If we progress on the path of emotional maturity, our loveliness and wisdom grow apace and more and more we become our best self, carried away in a flow of success. We 'get over' both ourselves and our commitment to littleness, learning that they are opposite sides of the same false coin.

We will learn to value our peace as the gateway to love, health, happiness and abundance. We will recognize that behaviors are either loving or calls for help. We will eventually give up blame and then judgment, not only to win our life back but to empower ourselves and those around us. Our life will grow in beauty and harmony and we learn to bless and lead the way for increase, rather than judge and lead the way to suffering. We make fewer naive mistakes and yet become more and more guileless. We recognize that our innocence and that of others are cut from the same cloth. Either we are both innocent and responsible or we are both guilty and punish ourselves. The path of emotional maturity is the path to Heaven on earth. It is the pathway back to the Beloved and the Heaven that it brings. The path of emotional maturity becomes ever lighter on the way home. And as we grow, our mind unifies and our friends join in community.

This book contains a gathering of some of the main principles of emotional integrity. Each of these lessons contains at least one principle. If we learn them, they will make us happy. They will help us to understand life and relationships and they will help us grow up emotionally. These principles help our relationships and our family and we become more attractive and easier to get along with. They will take us on a journey of understanding our own and others' emotions, transforming our relationships while preparing us to understand more of our subconscious mind and how it works. Making our subconscious conscious empowers us to make better choices and be more inclusive.

With emotional maturity, we become quick to see our part in any situation and become the first to apologize for mistakes and move the situation forward. With emotional maturity, we give up our need to win, to prove our superiority and have things our way. We begin to win success for ourselves and those around us. We restore our own and others' value and we become treasured as a team player. And, most of all, our happiness benefits all.

This journey of emotional maturity takes us to wholeness, and what we achieve we naturally share. As we attain emotional maturity, we open our hearts, feel more love and joy, and are naturally able to receive more. Our heart is not clogged up with the traps, triggers and emotional time bombs that beset most people.

I had always wondered if the inspiration would come to me to write a sequel to *If It Hurts, It Isn't Love*. It was such a seminal book, meant to be the Bible of relationships. I didn't know if there would be another. One morning, after boarding a plane at 6:40 in the morning in Honolulu, about 40 minutes before take off and after putting away my carry-ons and sitting in my seat, I was finally told, "Write that book now!" So, instead of reading the morning paper as I was wont to do when I first get on a morning plane, I got pen and paper and was off and this book, the sequel to *If It Hurts, It Isn't Love*, began. What had become an inspiration out of many good ideas was now impelling me. I wrote all the way to Switzerland, and for the next day and a half before my first lecture I wrote furiously. That continued on and off throughout that trip and was my main project beside the workshops and lectures. That was two and a half years ago. I have finished five other books since then that were in various stages of completion but this book has become the one pushing for birth.

After a couple of years of writing chapters for this book, I realized that what I was writing was too big for one book and was meant to be a series. To write a book of 366 lessons, as I did in *If It Hurts, It Isn't Love*, would make a book that was too big for easy handling, especially since the lessons in this book, *Heaven on Earth – The Path of Emotional Maturity* are longer. This is the first volume of that series of books on emotional integrity.

If we want to be happy, then we must clean up our act, because without emotional maturity, our happiness will be difficult to have and even more difficult to keep.

It is important to know that even if you learn all of these principles, when your next conflict rises to the surface or the next fight with another occurs, all of these things tend to be forgotten. Defensiveness, righteousness and attack surface. We forget we are only fighting for the illusion of some self-concept we think is both real and who we are. We are revisiting a shrine we have dedicated to the ego. As we go forward, these traps become even more subtle, though the falls can be just as long on the way down. Recognize this is the nature of evolving and don't let it stop you from contributing what you came to contribute.

The good news about emotional evolution is that typically we begin to bust ourselves and move in the right direction quicker and quicker. We begin to heal ourselves by not using these painful events as an excuse to hide and not step forward to greater success and bonding. We accept, forgive and let go. We catch ourselves sooner. We realize we are off our centers. We stop attacking ourselves, to everyone's relief and betterment. We give up feeling sorry for ourselves and start healing ourselves. We realize Heaven walks with us. It is Heaven's *will* and our true will that we be free. And if Heaven wills that we be free, then there must be an easy way.

Do not beat yourself up or attack others. Simply get back on track. Center yourself. Realize it's always a story that you wrote and all the characters reflect parts of your mind. You can heal the hidden wishes of every waking dream, and the beliefs and self-concepts that drive the dream, through forgiveness and helping instead of judging. Give yourself a break and you will give others a break. Include yourself and you will include all others. Help others and you will help yourself. You can be a shining example of the light. You can bring Heaven to earth. You can be who you came to be. If you miss an opportunity and act out or indulge yourself emotionally, you now have the opportunity to succeed through healing. Every time you are wounded, if you realize you are making a mistake that you can correct, you immediately get your power back.

We will all be taxed by the issues and lessons that we are to face. It is the way things are. When you learn these principles you will have so much more peace and your life will be so much happier. These principles will liberate you to the extent that you embrace and apply them. Once you free yourself, it is easy to help others. Yet, it is crucial to know that until we reach Oneness all of the fractures in our mind will come up to be faced, along with all the emotions that came about during that fracture.

This book is written for synchronicity so you can have a problem and open the book to a certain page or call out one of the chapter numbers and turn to that chapter to gain insight into what would help the problem. This makes it fun as an awareness and healing tool.

Principles of Emotional Integrity

1. An emotion shows we have made a mistake by siding with our egos.
2. Emotions, whether expressed or kept inside, generate stress.
3. We are responsible for our emotions. No one but us can make us feel anything.
4. Emotions are indicators, showing an opportunity for healing and wholeness.
5. Emotions hide gifts within us.
6. Emotions block the gifts Heaven wants to give us.
7. Every emotion expresses a need. A need represents a split mind where we want both to have the need met and to not have it met for fear of losing our independence.
8. An emotion comes from a judgment.
9. An emotion is a finger of accusation, blaming another for what is happening to us.
10. An emotion states that we have been victimized by another and, as such, our emotion is part of a power struggle and an act of revenge.
11. All emotions are from the past. They are memories impacted with feeling that come up in the present. They are part of a pattern that is holding us back.
12. When we side with our egos time after time, we develop a hidden or not so hidden bad attitude. This eats away at us and may show itself as chronic problems in many areas of our lives, even if we hide this willfulness from ourselves.
13. Our emotions come from our choices. They come from judgments that we make about certain situations. We can react in the old way, the pattern set within us, or make a new choice for peace.

14. A major emotion shows a place where we are avoiding our purpose and our destiny.

15. We could choose to look through the ego's eyes or look at an emotion from Heaven's perspective. In the former we will experience pain and in the latter, peace and joy.

16. An emotion is a form of blackmail and an attempt to control unless it is used for healing.

17. An emotion is an attempt to frame another for our failure to choose the path of the higher mind and to share the gifts waiting for us. This would have saved another from acting out and would have saved us from suffering.

18. An emotion shows a place of lost bonding from the past. It comes from the separation and pain that came about when we chose to go independent, using traumas and painful events as our excuse to do so.

19. A place of lost bonding, and its emotions, comes from a choice in which we failed to keep the sacred promise of our purpose by helping another.

20. When we separated but made it look like someone did something to us, the emotions of hurt, loss, inadequacy, sadness, fear, resistance, neediness, rejection, guilt, judgment, dissociation, and sacrifice sprang up.

21. When we separated, we were looking for some kind of ego payoff, such as: doing something we wanted to do all along; not doing something we didn't want to do; having an excuse; hiding; trying to pay off guilt; running from our purpose; being right; protecting ourselves from what we feared; controlling ourselves or others; or doing things our way. But separation always contains a desire to break away and be independent as well as attack and self-attack. None of this will make us happy.

22. An emotion actually hides a place where we were hard-hearted. We could have helped but didn't. Our emotion is coupled with this type of dissociation and our hard-heartedness will set up painful patterns of scarcity out of guilt that we didn't help.

23. The emotions we experience when we feel victimized are the very ones inside the person who seems to victimize us. It is the price we pay for refusing to help.

24. The ego persuades us that the pain we suffer is worth the independence we will gain. It promises to get rid of the

emotion but merely dissociates it, so the emotion is still locked inside.

25. Emotions are part of a script we have written to prove we are really the good ones and others are the 'bad' ones.

26. Properly used, an emotion becomes a place for inner healing or transformational communication that leads to bridging with another instead of separation.

27. All judgment and blame hide our own guilt. We judge and blame others for our past mistakes. This exacerbates the guilt within and keeps us from the realization of our own and everyone's innocence.

28. Judgment separates us and we use it to make us superior to others. This puts us into a vicious circle of domination-submission.

29. Emotions are mistakes and mistakes can be corrected. They are illusions where truth, gifts and peace could be instead. This is what healing is.

30. Every emotion shows a misunderstanding on our part but by misunderstanding we feel misunderstood. When we have right thinking and right perception, we will have peace and confidence.

31. An emotion shows where we are caught with a monocular view of life. Every judgment imprisons us. Instead, we can be freed from the prison of judgmental perspective that is based on our own guilt. We do this by making the choice to heal that leads to inspiration, guidance and creativity.

32. An emotion reflects a conflict within us that we frequently project outward.

33. Emotions are what problems are made of. When emotions are healed, there is peace and the problem is resolved. Emotional integrity is the foundation that can be used to understand and heal problems.

34. Emotions are a place of attack and self-attack. They are also an attack on ourselves as spirit and on God.

35. An emotion is the price we are willing to pay for independence. Yet the independence is not freedom but is a role that is tied to victim and sacrifice roles.

36. An emotion supports our egos. It is part of a dark story supported by the self-concepts that we thought would bring some kind of gain. Emotions and beliefs build the ego.

37. Emotions do not only affect us.
38. Emotions and victim situations are acts of revenge that express anger at others by attacking ourselves.
39. Emotions make walls between us and others.
40. Emotions block inspiration, guidance and the calls for help around us.
41. Emotions keep us feeling lonely and inadequate.
42. Emotions are an attempt to control.
43. Emotions are an attempt to bully or blackmail.
44. An emotion begs for attention and seeks specialness.
45. Emotions show a split mind.
46. Emotions, no matter how small, disturb our peace and could be exchanged for peace.
47. Emotions are a crossroads at which we will either compound the original mistake or use the situation to help ourselves and others while at the same time healing in a way that unifies.
48. Emotions are misunderstandings that show where we feel misunderstood.
49. Emotions show a place where we are afraid of the next step and where we feel guilty.
50. Emotions are an opportunity to heal and, as a result generate more love and success.
51. Emotions are part of a pattern that attracts similar emotions to it.
52. Emotions hide a better way.
53. Emotions declare that an injustice has been done to us and we use it to deny both God's presence and ourselves as the Child of God. Emotions are investments in littleness that deny our greatness.
54. Every emotion we have also carries the emotion of guilt with it, so if we do not heal our pain we begin to punish ourselves for all our emotions, including loss, rejection, fear, frustration, heartbreak, etc.
55. Our emotions and the experience of being a victim are an expression of anger at another that begins with attack on ourselves. It is also an attempt to pay off guilt that only succeeds in exacerbating it.
56. What we see others doing to us that 'causes' our emotions is actually what we are doing. Our emotions come from us and what we do. For instance, when we see someone

rejecting us, the emotion of rejection is coming from us rejecting them. This is the nature of projection, an ego defense to deny responsibility. This includes anger, and feelings of being unwanted or abandoned. It is what we decide that sets up our emotions.

Chapter 1

The Biggest Problem in Life and Relationships

The biggest problem in life is the same as that in relationships: we think that happiness is outside us and so we think that others were put on the earth to take care of our needs and to be the source of our happiness. In relationships, this can lead to fights, expectation, demands, competition, withdrawal, etc. In life it can lead to pain and grave disappointments. Expecting life or others to meet our needs leads to scarcity and frustration. It puts us into an attitude of taking rather than receiving, and this sooner or later brings about hurt and heartbreak. Many times, our taking is disguised as a form of giving. So if you gave a lot but felt hurt, you were giving to take.

As I heard one woman interviewer say to me on the phone, "Well, he should love me. He's my boyfriend." When I tried to explain how this wouldn't work because it was both an expectation and demand, she stated adamantly that that was the way it was supposed to be. She had set up roles and rules for how a relationship and a boyfriend should be and wouldn't listen to reason about how her rules were begging to be broken. She simply wasn't open to hearing any way different to what she imagined, and was behaving like most people who are caught in the heartbreak, win-lose stage of growth. Unfortunately, people at that stage tend to learn the hard way.

To look for your happiness outside yourself implies lack and need. This sets up an attitude of getting and taking. Need implies that a loss has occurred, and the attachment that comes from need leads again and again to sadness and pain.

The more healed you become, the more whole you are and, as a result, you stop seeking outside yourself for your happiness.

Chapter 2

Emotions are a Call for Help

Emotions are a call for help and are uncomfortable and painful. The message that comes consistently from your emotions is that you need the help of those around you. If your or others' behavior is not the behavior and experience of love, then it is a call for love.

Let's face it, everyone needs help and, when you are upset or in pain, you are really asking for help, even if that wasn't your conscious intention. Look around you and see who is calling for your help. Who is it that needs your support right now? Can you send them love? When you are upset, it is important to remember to support yourself also. If you don't have compassion for yourself, you will not see when others need your help. Anything that isn't love is a call for love.

Chapter 3

If You Are Feeling Bad, You Are Making a Mistake

If you are feeling bad, you are making a mistake. Others may be making a mistake but you are not in charge of them. If you start going down the path of controlling others, even if you are right you will be wrong. You may win the battle of feeling better momentarily, but you will lose the war. Trying to get others to change to make yourself feel better will work if you are a skilled communicator or a controller or a bully, but only the first one of these behaviors has integrity. Only communication is not a reaction, defense or manipulation. Only communication has the hope of healing the conflict in you so you achieve wholeness and do not have to face this problem once more.

If you are feeling bad, you are making a mistake. It may be one that was made a long time ago and you are getting a chance to choose again to make the right choice. You get a chance to clear something all the way from its roots up to the present. But if you don't realize when you feel bad that you are making a mistake and are called to change, you won't have the emotional integrity necessary to build partnership. You also won't be a friend to yourself. You will judge people where you have made a similar mistake. You will reject these people and reject once again those hidden or not so hidden parts in yourself.

If you are feeling bad, you are making a mistake. If you acknowledge your mistake, you are open to learn. If you acknowledge your mistake, your higher mind immediately begins to look for alternatives to correct it. So, as soon as you begin to feel bad in any way, whether it is reactive, depressive or rejecting, know that it is a mistake. It shows a place of separation between two parts of your own mind and it also means that it is a place of separation between you and others and it is typically well-defended. This is not helpful for your ability to respond.

Any problem, fight, conflict or defensiveness shows a mistake on *your* part. If you acknowledge your mistake, you have taken the first step in correcting it. Without this step, you may be caught in interminable defense and attack while attempting to justify or rationalize your stance. Why would you defend something that would keep you stuck in denial or later regretting your behavior? The need that is part of every bad feeling is an attempt to get or take and this is an attack. The ego is made up of attack and self-attack.

If you feel bad, you are making a mistake. You will either choose to change yourself, and thus take a step on the path of emotional maturity, or you will attempt to change others to suit yourself. If you attempt to change others so you can feel better. I wish you luck. If you choose to correct your mistake, grace awaits you. You could keep choosing peace instead of what you have been feeling. Layer by layer this corrects the mistake. Realize that if you are feeling bad, it is already an accusation that another is making you feel this way. It is a message to them that they should change. So, if you are feeling bad, there is already a mistaken choice but you can choose again and set things right. Your emotion is the accusation that most people are not aware of. The person being accused may be nowhere around, or even long dead, so it is manipulation to attempt to have them change by making them feel guilty about your emotions.

If you feel bad, take responsibility for the mistake you are making and change it. If you really want someone else to change, then the only effective way to accomplish that is to change yourself. Your inner conflict is expressed in an outer conflict with another and, if you change, both of you will be moved forward.

Chapter 4

If You Are Feeling Bad, It Is Your Responsibility

If you are feeling bad, it is your responsibility. If you are to be emotionally mature then taking responsibility is a natural part of that. If you do not take responsibility, you will be reactive. The more reactive you are, the more emotionally immature you are and the harder it is for others to be around you. You will wear out those around you, holding them hostage to your emotional reactions. Your emotional reactions can be a torture for others. When you react emotionally, you usually have no awareness of the effect on those around you because our emotional reactions typically obsess us. Your lack of awareness is your lack of responsiveness. Because you are not aware, it is easy to hurt, use, bully or offend. If you are not responsive, you become a taker instead of a giver. You will follow the path of upset instead of the path of peace. You think you are justified in feeling this way but you don't realize that you are actually polluting the emotional space of others. When you suffer, you don't suffer alone. When you change yourself for the better, it affects people in a healthy and helpful way but it needs you to take yourself in hand. Remember that when you feel bad it shows that you have already made the mistake, unless you are using it for healing. Otherwise, your emotion is broadcasting attack, usually unbeknownst to you but no less abusive.

Every upset shows a place you made a mistake. Now you can take responsibility for that mistake and correct it. If you don't take responsibility for it, who will? If you take responsibility, it is a step in maturity. If you blame, attack, project or emote as a form of emotional blackmail and attack, you are simply choosing to delay your learning and healing as well as your ability to partner. You might as well take every emotion as an opportunity to mature to a new level.

Choose wisely in how you use your emotions as there will be repercussions; you will reap what you sow.

Now is the time to commit to your emotional intelligence. How you do that is by committing to being responsible for your emotional experience. If you want to play a bigger game and be more mature, take responsibility for everyone around you. This makes you able to respond to others, knowing that they mirror your mind. You need your emotional responsiveness and so do others. The world is looking to birth itself to interdependence. This will occur when a certain critical mass has reached emotional maturity and thus partnership. So your emotional maturity is not just for your personal happiness, it is also for the happiness of those around you and the whole planet. Think of yourself as a happy, healthy cell on the body of planet earth. How you choose to be and act affects everyone, especially those around you. Your choice for emotional maturity will be a choice for your happiness. Unless you would like to follow the path of blind immaturity, I would suggest your continued commitment to responsibility for your own emotions and even for those you see around you. Response ability replaces guilt, including the guilt that hides under judgment, blame and condemnation. If you free yourself of guilt, you free everyone.

Chapter 5

You Are Never Upset for the Reason You Think

You are never upset for the reason you think. First of all, your ego, the principle of separation, is intent on obfuscation because if you saw what it was really up to, you would disown it. And this is the last thing the ego wants; it wants you to identify with it so it will survive. While the ego banks on its ability to misdirect, there may also be a number of layers to any particular problem. This means that when one layer is healed the next layer pops up as if no healing, or very little, had occurred. The ego wants us to go off half-cocked and fired up, blaming another or at the very least mistaking what is really going on.

The next time you get upset and think you know what is going on, just reflect for a moment that you might not have a clue as to what is actually occurring. Look back on other times when you thought you knew what was going on. How much did you actually realize what was going on at conscious, subconscious, unconscious and spiritual levels? There are so many intricacies of the mind occurring at all those levels. Learning and healing are ongoing on the path of a golden life and beyond. The more righteous and convinced you are of your position, the more your defenses demonstrate that you are hiding something that you consider too sensitive to deal with, and so it is no wonder you run from it. No one wants to suffer. The ego volunteers to help with that through dissociation, repression and splitting parts of the mind off. It is not crucial to know where the problem is coming from to heal it. Simply forgive yourself and everyone involved time and time again. Each time you will become more peaceful until you finally reach a place of profound peace.

Chapter 6

All Upset Comes From the Past

Anything that upsets you comes from your past. An old cache of pain has somehow been triggered in the present. There are enough similarities in the current situation that it brings up the old upset, hurt or anger. If you realize that much of what is not happy for you is what you are bringing in from your history, then it allows you to take some of the people that you have been judging and attacking in the present off the hook. This allows you to be more empathetic to those around you and even allows you to be more compassionate toward yourself.

Bringing the past into the present is an old notion in the healing profession. In psychiatry, it's called transference. If something occurs in your life that is not happy, it's transference. In Gestalt therapy, it's called unfinished business but it shows that those in the healing profession have been aware of this dynamic for a long time. The awareness of this principle can help you to take responsibility for whatever appears around you in your life now.

When I discovered this back in the 1970s, I developed the intuitive method as a way to find where the roots of an issue came from. I would ask people to examine one of their big problems and ask themselves, "If I were to know when this began, it was probably at the age of...

Later, when the unconscious started to intrude, I began to ask, "If you were to know, did this begin before, during or after your birth? ... If it occurred before your birth, if you were to know was it in the womb or before? It was probably..." If the answer was before, I would ask, "If you were to know whether it is ancestral or soul level, it's probably..." If it was ancestral, I would ask if it was from mother's, father's or both sides of the family.

I found many ways to heal these patterns but one way is to ask what gift they had brought in to heal the family. I would then have them open up that door in their mind where that soul gift resided, fill themselves up with it energetically, then send it back through their mother's, father's or both sides of the family.

If the problem began at a soul level, I would ask them, if they were to know, in which lifetime did the pattern begin, and in which country. I would ask if they were a man or a woman in that lifetime, and finally if they were to know, what happened back there and how it's affecting them now. Sometimes I would ask what gift or purpose they were afraid to embrace at that time that had caused the problem. Then I would have them embrace it now and send it back through their lifetimes, or through their unconscious to that story if they preferred that metaphor. This removes the pattern and allows life a better way.

Chapter 7

If You Are Feeling Bad, You Are in Conflict

If you are feeling bad, it means that you are in conflict. There is a way that you could have peace instead. The conflict within you may spill out to a conflict in your world. This means that there are at least two different parts of your mind that want two opposite things, like wanting peace and drama or wanting commitment and independence. This puts you at odds with yourself and makes you feel bad. You are 'at sixes and sevens' as the old saying goes and at war with yourself. So, if you are ever feeling bad and don't know the reason, it has to do with an inner conflict. With any problem in your life, you are feeling upset but what opposes you in the problem reflects the less identified side of your mind.

Healing, which is both a step forward and a new level of wholeness, always has to do with some form of integrating. Integration is when you take two different parts of your mind and melt them together into a new whole. This brings peace, more bonding, greater strength and a new flow. An integration can occur with two negative parts, a positive and a negative, or two positive parts of your mind. When an integration occurs, what is negative is turned around and transformed into the positive, adding more confidence to your life. When two positives are integrated, the positive is multiplied.

There are many ways to integrate in a conflict. Integrations come about by identifying the parts that are split and imagining them in front of you, melting down to their pure light and energy and then coming together. Bring the new wholeness and light into you. Alternately, you could ask Heaven to bring these parts together or you yourself could simply choose that this occurs. All of these forms of integration will work if you want them to.

Chapter 8

Emotions Come From Conflict

Emotions signal that you are in conflict. This means that at least two parts of your mind and sometimes more are not in accord. You want two opposite things and are being pulled apart by the conflict. It seems to you that you want only one thing. You want the success; you don't want the loss or the heartbreak but the subconscious tells a different story. This is why it's subconscious. It doesn't tell the same story that you are consciously telling yourself and others. Some people go to great lengths of anger and denial at the mere suggestion that they wanted something other than what their emotions are lamenting. Yet, if you only want one thing, then that is what occurs. If you are wholehearted and your mind is whole, then that is what occurs. Your pain suggests conflict. You regain your power when you bring to light and then to truth the hidden parts of your mind. You cannot heal something or make another choice when you hide something from yourself. Your awareness gives you your power back. You are so much less likely to make bad decisions if you know the whole picture of what you are choosing.

Your emotions show and testify to you and everyone else what you thought you wanted. The results show that you actually wanted something else. The subconscious, even in the direst situations, shows a conflict with the side you have hidden and identify with least. This is the side you hide from yourself. This does not mean that it is the weakest side because, if you are suffering, that side had its way even at the cost of you suffering.

It is true to welcome to the surface what you hid from yourself because only then can the situation be resolved. Only then can you make a more enlightened choice in which you don't seem to get blindsided or sabotaged.

Want with all your heart to see what you have hidden from yourself. On the surface, you are upset because someone didn't live by your script. But at a deeper level, they exactly acted out your script. Every time you suffered, this was what was going on. You can look back at past events and through your determination and intuition find your hidden script and what you were trying to get as a result. When your desire gets stronger than your fear, your mind reveals what you hid from yourself.

Remember to commit to your innocence. Everyone has made mistakes and to know your mistakes is to correct them. The ego will attempt to have you take the blame you have put on others. If you begin to explore your deeper mind and put the blame back on yourself, you are just as trapped in illusion as when you blame another. But judgments, blame, grievances and guilt all show that you haven't fully seen or understood what is happening. When you see and understand the whole situation, you will both experience peace and get your power back. This is the best time to decide what you really want.

Chapter 9

Every Upset Reflects an Opportunity

One of the things that can help when you are feeling bad is to recognize the place of opportunity that you are in. First of all, this event is an opportunity for healing. If, in spite of what is going on that is painful, you commit to healing then healing stays uppermost in your mind throughout the experience.

Know that there is another way of looking at an event that leads to peace and that this peaceful perspective is the true way to look at it. If you keep getting hurt, angry or feel more depressed, know that you are going in the wrong direction and it is in your hands as to whether you will achieve peace or not. Commit to your healing. This will restore your innocence and wholeness. Don't stop until you find the way that gives you a true perspective. There is a way to have peace. This is the best way to look at any upsetting circumstance, as peace is the foundation of love, abundance and happiness. There is another way to look at an event that brings largesse and opportunity. Don't stop asking for the perspective of peace. Choose for it to come to you and ask for your higher mind, as it is this mind that has answers as opposed to your ego mind.

Chapter 10

Emotions are a Form of Attack

Emotions are a form of attack. While emotions seem to come up spontaneously from within or as a result of being triggered by something outside, at a deeper level they are meant to attack someone around you, someone from the past, and God. Emotions began as a result of lost bonding in the past where you were attacking instead of helping, though you have told yourself and others, it was others attacking you. That premise holds only on the surface of the mind. Your emotions are the fruits of separation and, though they may have started a long time ago, they are now used to keep the separation going. When emotions come out, they attack someone in the present and someone from the past once again.

The ego is separation. And the foundation of the ego is attack and self-attack. Left to themselves, your emotions attack those around you and, unless they are responding with compassion to your emotions, they will experience attack. If you see your and others' emotions as an indication of something you need to heal as well as another's call for help, you will use your emotions as an opportunity for transformation. This can heal your pain and your conflicts giving you greater confidence and more natural flow.

Today, you can transform any of your emotions rather than use them for attack. Put your emotions in Heaven's Hands layer by layer until you are experiencing peace once more. Be aware when you are experiencing anything less than happiness. Ask what you are using your emotions for and who they are attacking. Then choose again to use your emotions for healing and put them in Heaven's Hands.

Chapter 11

Emotions are a Form of Self-Attack

Emotions are a form of self-attack. Emotions feel bad unless you are using them for healing. Then there is the experience of the emotion, as well as birth. The moment of healing is poignant with sweet release.

With emotions, one part of you doesn't want to feel bad and is utterly dismayed to suffer in this way, while the other part is almost gleeful in its attack on you. It tells you things that you and others have said. "Who do you think you are?", "You got what you deserve", "You, Stupid!", "That was the biggest mistake of your life!" are just a few of the things you attack yourself with, not to mention how others may have attacked you verbally. What others attack you with is a hidden form of self-attack. Emotions come from a conflict where two parts of your mind attack each other, each trying to defeat the other.

The ego gets fat on self-attack. It propagates self-attack because it is one of its two major building blocks – the other is attacking others. The ego always wants you to feel some emotion so it keeps you in enough pain to feed itself. Your ego does not have your best interest at heart. It builds itself with self-aggrandizement, specialness and competition, as well as with the impatience and anger that goes with these. It also promotes smallness and even self-abasement so you can hide, feel fearful, inadequate and unworthy. The ego is a conglomeration of self-exaggeration and self-deflation, adding up to a split-mind and a Littleness Conspiracy. When you are upset or in pain, it is good to repeat the words from *A Course in Miracles*, "I won't condemn myself for this", until you are at peace.

Chapter 12

Emotions are a Defense

Now is the time to give up using your emotions as a defense and commit to defenselessness. Using pain as a defense is your attempt at safety. Using pain to protect you from pain cannot be a good defense because you suffer in order not to suffer. This is typical ego logic that only works for the ego if unexamined. Once you realize what you've hidden from yourself, you make a better choice. There has to be a better way. Pain as a defense only begets more pain. If you move beyond your emotions to peace, your pain and your story about how it came about will transform into a happier story.

Emotions spring up because there is something you cannot accept. Emotions are your protest. They are your complaint. Your emotions scream that an injustice has been committed but this is not the ultimate truth, which is why it can be healed. It is only something you cannot accept. If you accept it, it is let go of. It is no big thing. Instead of stopping you, what has occurred is let go of and falls into perspective. You are back in the flow. If you accept it all the way into your mind, integration occurs and a new wholeness begins. This brings peace and confidence where there once was pain and fear. Now you can go on once more. Your faith has been restored. Emotions refuse to go on. They are a defense against what is happening. Emotions are the fight against what is and as a result you keep on suffering. Only when acceptance occurs can you go on. You do not have to like something to accept it. If you don't accept it as it is, you will never get beyond it. With acceptance, your emotions bring release and then poignancy.

Chapter 13

Emotions Show Where You Were Afraid of Your Power

Emotions show where you were afraid of your power. They actually show where you separated from others, yourself, the Divine and your power. You became more frightened of yourself, your greatness and your purpose. You became more willful and unwilling, more dissociated and independent, more attacking and self-attacking.

The extent to which you are afraid of your power, is the extent to which you become a victim and pretend to others and yourself that you are not responsible for what happens to you. It is this repression of your collusion that keeps your charade of powerlessness in place. You have no conscious idea that it is your choice; part of a script that you write for certain purposes. So whenever you have emotions, you have given up the power that comes of bonding. You have followed the ego's plan of attack and not that of Heaven or your higher mind. You went for independence, control, attack, domination and submission when you didn't go for the power of your gifts, purpose and destiny that reflects the path of the higher mind.

It is now time to assume your power. As you forgive and heal the dark emotions, you become more willing to shine with the power of your gifts, purpose, destiny and the light within you.

Chapter 14

Emotions Speak of Loss

Emotions speak of loss. You have emotions because bonding has been broken. Whether that occurred in the present moment or from something that emerged from the past, emotions can only spring up when loss has occurred. The loss you experience calls you to let go of the attachment you favor, so that in the letting go there is a new beginning. Now is the time to let go and reconnect. You experienced the loss because you stopped valuing what it was you lost and you went for greater independence. Now you can realize your loss and let go of the attachment, loneliness and resistance that sprang up in its place. You withstand the pain so you can separate, but letting go allows you to get over the loss and move forward once again. As you let go, the need that comes up with loss is able to be fulfilled, but while there is attachment and holding on your need cannot be met. Emotions tell you where there is something in your life that needs to be let go of because if you don't do so, you are stuck. Holding on keeps you in a place of scarcity. Holding on is meant to compensate for the loss but it keeps you experiencing the loss. When your emotions have turned to peace, then the loss has been transcended and you are in the flow once more.

Now is the time for you to ask yourself who or what you are still holding onto. As you let go of the attachment to the past, you are brought back to the present where you can receive once more.

Chapter 15

Suppression of Emotion is a Mistake

Suppression of emotion is a mistake. It adds stress to your life and you still carry the feeling inside even though you don't feel the intensity of it any longer.

While at one level all emotion lacks integrity, to suppress emotion is to not give voice to your experience. Even if your experience is mistaken, which an emotion shows, it is a bigger mistake to suppress it. This doesn't give you an excuse to use your emotions to bully or blackmail others, but it does mean to give voice to them so that they can be healed. If you do not express your anger, it will tax you and others around you.

The principle is not to suppress the emotion, but to recognize and use it for healing as soon as you are no longer in the throes of it. This means to apologize where necessary after you have attacked directly or indirectly with your emotion, and to become more aware of your unfolding process and your emotions. A balance is needed between expressing and containing your emotion. The problem with suppressing emotion is that it keeps you from knowing what needs healing. It is certainly better to heal than just rant. Commit to know your emotions; commit to transform them so they become the gifts and wholeheartedness they were meant to be.

Chapter 16

Be Not Afraid

Fear is a by-product of judgment and separation. Every time we lose bonding more fear is created. Subconsciously, despite how the situation may look, whenever bonding was lost, we were looking to be independent. This separation split our mind and both conflict and separation lead to fear. Judgment, which is an attempt to be separate and superior to what is being judged, is a form of attack. Whatever we are doing we see others and the world doing to us. So, when we are attacking we experience the world attacking us and we are afraid.

At the root of every problem there is fear. At the root of all defenses there is fear. Where we are independent there is the dissociation we use to hide our dependency, which contains need, fear, heartbreak and guilt. Independence is a role; it prevents receiving and is actually frightened to receive. Fear is the core negative emotion; upon it all the other emotions will be built. If you find anything other than happiness, you will find some degree of fear.

In the Bible one phrase is used more than any other. It is, "Be not afraid" or "Fear not". There must be a good reason that this is so. Love is the opposite of fear. It extends itself rather than shrinks or stays frozen. This creates flow. There are other things that heal fear, such as willingness, bonding, acceptance, forgiveness, letting go, joining, integration, peace, bridging, truth, communication, commitment, creativity and helping others, to name but a few. All of these help us know that fear is not something we are stuck with. Since the ego is made of fear, to say "Be not afraid" is to say, "Be not of your ego". Some of the most violent people are frightened, paranoid people.

A *Course in Miracles* tells us that if we knew Who walked beside us we could never be afraid. This encourages us to keep up our spiritual awareness. If every problem hides fear, think who you could love today to help heal both their fear and your hidden fear. Because love will heal your fear. Be not afraid to love and help others. Be not afraid! Remember Who walks with you.

Chapter 17

Emotions Communicate at Subconscious Levels

Emotions communicate at both conscious and subconscious levels, and they communicate all kinds of messages. Many of them are general but some are quite specific. One common message of emotions is the victim message: "Look what you did to me." Another frequent message is: "Please help me" or "Please love me". Emotions may be a call for attention or they may be an attempt to get your needs met. Emotions may be a warning, such as: "Don't do this!" or "Don't you be like me!" The messages of emotions may be part of a fight or even express hope or hopelessness. They may be expressing love through the pain, which is a form of sacrifice or martyrdom.

The best way to discover these messages is to write down the key people that we give these subconscious messages to, such as mother, father, siblings, partner, ex-partners, self, God, friends, work associates, and anyone else who comes to mind. Then, using your intuition, ask yourself what message you were giving to each of these people.

When you have the answer to these questions, you will have the subconscious dynamics of what brought the emotion about. Then you can heal these dynamics by communicating consciously, forgiving, letting go, etc. in order to transform these emotions and be free.

Chapter 18

Emotions Give Us Dissociated Independence

Emotions are the expression of lost bonding, both past and present. They are dissociated by the ego as part of its deal to get rid of the pain of separation. But the ego does not get rid of these emotions; it only succeeds in hiding them from your awareness by dissociation. This buries the emotions inside you, because the ego uses this pain to build its walls. It hides pain making it less available to your healing. This cuts you off from your heart and your compassion. When you are insensitive to yourself, you become insensitive to others. When your mind is split from the lost bonding that occurred, you lose touch with yourself. You are not just independent from others and from Heaven, you are also independent from your true will and what is best for you. The more independence grows within you, the more willful you become. You do things that don't serve you or your well-being. One common aspect of this is using what would have been miracle energy for sex. This comes from willfulness on your part and you miss the manifold fulfillment that would have come to you and others through the transcendence a miracle brings.

To be independent is to have a split-mind and the extent that your mind is split is the extent that you are stuck. Your dissociated independence keeps you from receiving, which is having the natural reward and recognition for what you do and what you give.

It is important to realize that when you are in dissociation you are stuck, and the only real way out is to regain your heart and your feminine side. Otherwise you will burn yourself out and never reach full partnership with a significant other, yourself and Heaven.

Chapter 19

Emotional Pain is the Price You Pay for Independence

Emotions are the price you pay for independence. I am not speaking of the independence that is the natural maturity that evolves from your dependent child stage. I am speaking of the dissociated independence that comes about when you have dark things happen to you. Chosen consciously and repressed, or chosen subconsciously, the desire for independence is ego-driven and leads to pain. You hope to become masters of your own fate with the independence of the ego but when you break bonding, you suffer. You cannot easily tear yourself away from someone you are bonded to. You must blame another for the broken bonding, projecting out your guilt for breaking away and not helping others when you could have saved the day. You pay a price for independence. When you take on the role of independence through emotion, you also take on victim and sacrifice roles. Like all roles, it is dissociated; it can neither receive nor enjoy what comes to it. It is a defense that comes from judgment and it is meant to compensate for feelings of failure and guilt.

So, the breaking of bonding splits you into independence, sacrifice and victim roles. The extent of a person's independence shows the degree of loss-neediness, hurt, heartbreak and guilt-unworthiness they have inside. Dependence, our victim side, can also have a hidden independent or inadvertent victimizer side that is waiting for an excuse to come out and take over.

Knowing this may allow you to make a true choice when you are at the crossroads and deciding whether to go toward your ego and its independence, or toward your gifts. Make enough choices toward truth and it becomes second nature, avoiding the pain you pay unnecessarily in order to have false independence.

Chapter 20

All Emotions are Illusions

All emotions are illusions. It is not illusion that you feel emotion, because you certainly do. Yet, at the deepest quantum physics or spiritual level all is light or 'the dream'. Emotion is illusion in that it is not the most essential level. At the deepest level, there is love and peace, wholeness and innocence. This is why all emotion can be healed, because it is not the truth except as you experience it. As a result you are not stuck with what you are feeling; you can change it. There are many ways to transform an emotion but the important, first step is to realize as soon as you can that negative emotions are not just mistakes you make, they are illusions you invest in.

This can be challenging in the heat of anger, heartbreak or depression. But if you set your mind to it, it is much easier to catch yourself if you realize that you are not just experiencing an illusion, you are also investing in pain. Knowing that emotions are not the truth can open your mind to find healing alternatives to situations that you are caught in. If you are stuck in any problem, it also means there are emotions involved that you are stuck in.

Jung made the distinction between emotions, which are negative, and feelings, which are positive. I follow his classification but will specify when I use them in a different way such as 'positive emotions' or 'negative feelings'.

The next time an emotion strikes say to yourself: "This is not the truth, I want the truth and only the truth." Don't stop making this declaration until you have reached the place of peace that becomes joy. Your intention would have taken you from illusion to the truth and how you feel will be the measure of that.

Chapter 21

Under Every Problem is a Gift

Under every problem there are hidden emotions. The problem is the outer expression of the emotion and the conflict within. But if you are not afraid to address the emotion, if you are not cowed by the fear of your dark feelings, you can feel them and pass through the emotion to the gift within that is hidden by the problem. The size of the problem shows the size of the gift. The bigger the problem, the bigger the gift.

The emotions were actually a price you were willing to pay rather than have the gift. This sounds back to front until you realize most people actually have a fear of shining and a fear of success. The gift that awaits you would make you shine; it would make you stand out in the crowd because of your brightness. To embrace this gift you would have to give up a certain amount of control, something your ego never wants to do. With a gift there is flow and a level of generosity and engagement that melts the ego. The gift gives you confidence while your ego gives you control.

Some people have the courage to feel through their emotions to the gift, bringing a new level of wholeness. Others have the courage to intuit and embrace the gift, which then transcends the emotions as the light and relatedness of the gift are embraced.

Notice a problem you have. Would you like to get past it? If you would, decide whether you would like to go through the emotions to the gift or embrace the gift outright to transcend the emotions. If you choose the path of feeling your emotions, one of the benefits is that you become braver around experiencing them. This also allows you to win back parts of your heart that you lost to both negative emotions and hard-heartedness. Winning back your heart gives you greater capacity for joy and the ability to receive. It also gives you a greater capacity to partner.

If you are willing to follow the path of healing emotions, ask that the emotions that have been part of what was a hidden problem come out, so that you can become aware of them. When they do, simply feel them. Lean into your emotions. Feel them aggressively. Go for it. You may want to ask for Heaven's help or have your angel hold you as you do this. Ask that these feelings come out at a rate that you can deal with them easily. Lean into these emotions until you feel that the emotions no longer disturb you and the problem is no longer an obstacle. Then keep going until you reach the level of peace that dissolves the problem.

If you choose the path of intuiting the gift, ask with all your heart what that gift is. Ask that when you recognize the gift, you know with all of your being that **this is the gift**. It may come in a dream, a vision; you may see it in someone around you, even on TV or in a book. Embrace that gift. Own it as your own. Feel it surging through you. Share it energetically with everyone both around you and in your problem situation. Then go back through your life to anyone who seems as if they could use this gift and share it with them.

Chapter 22

Emotions Make You Independent but It's Not What You Hoped For

Emotions make you independent but it's not what you hoped for. What you hoped for was freedom. What you hoped for was truth. What you hoped for was adventure and doing things your way. Independence frightens you so you never become completely independent. You were hoping to fulfill some kind of fantasy that you thought would make you happy. But fantasies don't make you happy; only reality makes you happy. By breaking bonding you suffered emotions and experienced one set of illusions, in this case the pain of the victim and its neediness and dependency, in exchange for another set of illusions that seemed to give you freedom and power. This event also brought another role, that of sacrifice, and all three roles added to your feelings of deadness, your dissociation and inability to receive and enjoy. Your independence tends to gather more dependent people around you who mistake your dissociation and not caring for confidence. It also makes you frightened of your neediness and dependency when you want to possess another person for your happiness. Now you run from those who want to possess you. You defend against the neediness and sacrifice within you that are projected out on others who are attempting to possess you.

Independence is not what it's cracked up to be because the dissociation of independence is a loss of heart. You defend against the emotion that made you independent but you also cut off your heart from feeling, truth and partnership. You cannot enjoy life because you hardened your heart. To get your heart back, you must go through your emotions.

To find peace and love, you must go beyond the need for independence to interdependence, and heal the emotions still buried within. If your emotions and the independence are integrated, you will have reached a level of partnership and flow that contains greater truth and freedom.

Chapter 23

Do You Want to Feel or Be Dissociated?

You can feel all there is to feel or you can dissociate, but you can't do both. If you cut off your bad feelings, you also cut off the good. The best stance is to feel it all. If you do, it will make you first a lover, then a poet and finally a mystic. When the bad feeling is past, and it will pass if you don't hold on or run from it, there will be peace in its place. Peace gives you the ability to love. If you keep going you will become a poet, chronicling the passage of feelings and delights and finally loving it all. At that point, you become a mystic as well as a poet because Love lifts you to love even more.

Dissociation, on the other hand, is an attempt to not suffer and even to survive. But as in any defense, it ends up causing what it tries to save you from. Dissociation splits your mind. It makes you ambivalent and wishy-washy. It gives you two experiences at the same time, one of which you usually hide from yourself. It cuts off your heart and therefore your ability to receive, enjoy, partner and give yourself.

All. of these splits in your mind are conflicts that generate fear, pain and guilt. This is a trap in the form of independence. You blind yourself to avoid seeing that to get to the independence you want, you have to play the victim and sacrifice yourself. All of these roles render you unable to receive or feel worthy enough to have equality and partnership.

Dissociation is the ego's attempt to help you get rid of pain but it does this by locking it inside, pretending the pain is gone. This is not good for you but it is good for the ego as it builds itself in this very way.

Dissociation gives you a false sense of control and having it 'my way' but you end up sitting on a powder keg. These emotions cause stress and it takes a good bit of your life energy to keep them cut off. Life will generate bigger and bigger ways to jolt you, to try and get the pain out. This is not pleasant to say the least; it can feel like an attack or even an invasion. If you get defensive, you can exacerbate things and this makes for a difficult birth, a labor without merit and a lesson that becomes a trial. If, when these jolts occur you realize that it can be for the good, then you will recognize the emotions that pour forth as what is necessary to heal yourself and get the poison out of you. Otherwise, in an attempt to be right and dissociate even more, you will deny and become more self-important. The key is not to suffer but not to attempt to save yourself by dissociation either, because it won't work. The key is to release your emotions, invite them all out and heal them. This is not to say that you have a tantrum, which is the other side of the trap, and which means you would be using your emotions to attack.

Healing begins first with emotional release and then with the release of the judgment that is creating the suffering. If you judge rather than forgive, you hide your guilt under blame and you put pain on top of that and fear under it. Then you attempt to cover the whole mess by cutting it off. The chaos gets locked inside your mind.

Choose to be courageous. The emotions you build up inside lead to problems. They are toxic and can lead to injury or illness and you are heading in a death direction. Have the courage to feel. Emotions aren't endless. Even if you were to 'hit a gusher' by tapping into an unconscious pattern that takes you to your knees, you simply ask for Heaven's help. As you go through these feelings, they become a birth. The feeling of grace will grow, first as a trickle and then it will become the mainstream of your experience. As you concentrate on the grace, the emotion burns away even more quickly, becoming love. So buck up. Commit to feeling it all to win back your heart and your compassion. It will give you the lesson so you can share the wisdom to help others who have fallen into a similar trap. As you help them, subconscious and unconscious elements of your trap are released also.

In *A Course in Miracles*, it states that we have dissociated Heaven itself. Heaven is both exquisite bliss and love but also the awareness of Oneness. Have courage and commit today to uncover the biggest dissociation holding you back. Claim an easy birth. Ask for Heaven's help. Have the courage to feel whatever comes up. It is Heaven's Will that you get through this in the easiest possible way. Trust the process and you will move through it quickly. Commit to it and you will move through it even more quickly. Want the wholeness at the other end with all your heart. Don't let your emotions bully you and don't use dissociation as a way of running from your life. Feel it all. Your heart is worth it and so is your success.

Chapter 24

Emotions Make You a Victim

Emotions make you a victim. Emotion is both the effect of being victimized and it is what makes you a victim. In spite of what seemed to occur, subconsciously it was you that broke the bonding with life, another, yourself and Heaven. Yet, when you do so, in your forgetfulness you project out what you did on to another. You use your upset to prove that you have been hurt and someone else has done something to you and that they are the guilty party. If, during whatever ordeal you were undergoing, you kept your love and connection to others, life, yourself and Heaven without judgment, resistance or grievance, there would have been no pain and no victimization.

Your emotion is the signal and your 'evidence' that you have been victimized. It is the cry of complaint that life, another and Heaven has been unfair.

The key here is *not* to not have emotion. That would be suppression, repression and a denial of your experience. The key is to heal yourself when you do have emotion. It is crucial to your freedom that you give up the revenge and separation that were the hidden or not so hidden elements in the situation. This situation also included attack and self-attack, the foundation of the ego on a grand order. Emotions signal that **you did the separating** because you sided with your ego and now you can choose to bond once more by joining and forgiving. This reverses the victim pattern and heals the emotions as you choose not to blame others or yourself.

Chapter 25

Independence Hides Fear of the Next Step

Independence hides fear of the next step. All the busyness, or in some few cases the laziness, of independence is a cover for fear. Stress is the same. It's a decoy. All the pushing, control and deadness of independence are not what's really going on. They are signposts on the road that say you are afraid to go further. You are afraid of the intimacy and success. You attempt to make it convincing by having difficulty or working hard, but it's all camouflage. You are simply afraid of the next step. Your willingness to go forward cuts through your fear and allows you to move past this delay where you have frightened yourself.

When you are independent, it doesn't seem as if you are afraid of anything. But you are afraid of being possessed and captured by another. You are afraid of being oppressed. You are afraid of commitment. You are afraid you can't handle the intimacy and success of the next step so you make a big pretense of working for it while you are resisting it. You are afraid you can't handle your purpose and are afraid to shine, which is the necessary pre-requisite for your destiny. Get over your fear and you get over your illness. Get over your fear and you get over any problem you are stuck in, and thereby move to a new level of interdependence.

Chapter 26

Emotions Put You in Sacrifice

Emotions put you in sacrifice. It is not just that you feel bad when you experience the upset of emotions, which is actually unnecessary suffering and sacrifice, it is also that emotions signal the separation that leads to the role of sacrifice. All roles are ineffective in that they stop you from receiving in regard to whatever it is that you are doing. In that way, all roles are sacrifice. The role of sacrifice is especially ineffective in that anything done through sacrifice could be done without it.

The ego talks us into sacrifice as if it was the only way, as if it was a form of love, but sacrifice is doing the right thing for the wrong reason. It is competitive, a form of attack, and it generates feelings of deadness and burnout. Every role is a sacrifice, and you cannot receive while you employ sacrifice. It is a psychological mistake that somehow proves, at least to you, that you are morally ascendant both to those in the past who didn't take care of you better and also to those in the present.

When you experience emotions, it is important for you to make a course correction and get back on track. It is time for you to get centered and regain your peace. If you do not restore bonding then you are left with deadness or the soap opera of your emotions. All sacrifice covers over the pain of lost bonding but the pain is still there. It is time for you to restore the ease and flow of bonding by committing to equality time and again, until you reach high level equality with the people involved now. It is also crucial to commit time and again to equality with those you judged from the past as the judgment keeps the pattern of sacrifice going now.

Chapter 27

No One Can Make You Feel Anything

All of your emotions come from you. No one can make you feel anything you don't choose to feel. No one makes you angry. No one makes you sad. No one makes you feel guilty and no one hurts you. These emotions were already inside you waiting for the opportunity to be triggered and come out.

To say that someone makes you feel something is to say that they could unscrew your head, climb down inside you and hit the guilt button or the hurt button, pull back the throttle of anger, yank the chain of frustration or hit the switch of sadness. Even though others *seem* to make us feel something, our emotions come from our choice in regard to how to respond to what is before us. Certainly there are predilections within us that come from our past choices and the experiences that resulted from them, but we still get to choose each time – though some emotional reactions are so quick that it doesn't seem that way at all.

Our choices that lead to either response or reaction come about in a split second. Because they are so quick, you think that another made you angry or hurt you. Now is the time to become aware that you have a choice about how you want to think and respond, because this will set the experience in your mind and how it is for you.

You can take responsibility for your emotions and become aware that you dictate your emotions and not the other way around. If you have reacted rather than responded, you can begin the healing process to return to your center. Now is the time to win back your power. Choose now to have awareness in that split second of choice before you act. Decide now that you will fully witness what you decide, and how you react or respond accordingly. When you witness without judgment, even if you react, you will be empowered for whatever it is you truly want in the future. Witnessing breaks the bondage that you were caught in and gives you awareness of your choice and what effect it has. Awareness, choice and knowledge of the effects give you your power back.

Chapter 28

Your Emotional Experience Depends on How You are Using an Event

Your emotional experience depends on how you are using an event. If you are using it for healing then, in spite of any suffering or hardship, there is a desire for birth, a curiosity about what was really going on and an anticipation about the gifts that were hiding under the pain.

Most people do not know what emotion is truly for and so the ego hijacks an emotional event and holds you hostage to the pain. But in truth, an event will be used either in service to the ego or to the higher mind. The ego blandishes you with what cannot make you happy; it separates you from yourself and those you love. If you follow the ego, you do not follow the path of happiness. If you follow the higher mind, you neither run from emotion nor do you revel in it with guilt or self-pity. You understand that to go through the emotion as quickly as possible, trusting the process, brings you to a new birth. You know that, as a result of going through the emotion, the result will bring more of your heart back. The higher mind uses an event for learning and to make you whole again. It uses every emotional event as a way to step up, realize your power, achieve more peace and embrace the gifts, purpose and destiny that would transform the situation.

The ego attempts to use an emotional event to get needs met and gain attention. Yet, whatever you get, you don't feel quite satisfied with because you feel you had to strategize, albeit subconsciously, to get it. This way does not allow you to receive, only to *get*, which doesn't fulfill your needs. It only makes you hungrier. Getting and taking are the ego's solution to having needs met while still staying independent. The only things that really work for fulfillment are giving or receiving as these restore the bonding and fulfill you.

So, when emotions come up, and they will, give them to your higher mind. Let it be in charge and the upset will be used in the service of what builds your life.

Chapter 29

Let Your Contractions Be Birth Labor

Let your contractions be birth labor. If you are birthing then your contractions serve a purpose for life. If you are contracting because you are shrinking from pain, shock or disappointment, then it serves the ego's purpose and it steers you in a death direction.

I have worked with people who had so much pain and shock that they became a shadow of their former selves. This is when healing is called for. The ego wants you limited because it is made of limits and when you are limited it is strongest.

The key to turning contraction into birth rather than death is first to be aware when you are undergoing contractions. This sounds simple but when you are undergoing contractions, you tend to forget everything else because of the pain.

Whenever something untoward hits you, you can set your mind to remember to choose it as a means to birth at a whole new level. The ego will tell you it's time to die but you get to choose what part of your mind you will listen to: your ego or your higher mind. You determine your experience by your choices and you determine the meaning your experience has for you once it's occurred or even as it is occurring. Choose life. Choose birth now and for the time ahead.

Chapter 30

Getting Over Yourself is a Question of Attitude

Getting over yourself is a question of attitude. Being stuck on yourself, making yourself the center of the universe, comes with a certain amount of blindness. Being caught up in yourself is narcissism, a denial of love. You are simply unavailable for connection because (fanfare here!) life is all about you and how special you are. You are imprisoned in yourself, having to maintain the biggest idol there is, which is the idol of your own self-concept and who you think you are. Your ego needs a lot of upkeep and you must make sure that others treat you with the proper respect and honor that you accord yourself. You have become a legend in your own mind and others must treat you in a like manner or they are to be punished. Idols are always disappointing and the Idol of Self-Concepts is central to the whole pantheon of idols. Idols demand maintenance and their upkeep takes a lot of energy that would otherwise be used for joy. We think that they will save us, meet our needs and make us happy, but they don't.

I think of the painting of Narcissus from the Romance period. He is there at a pond surrounded by beautiful women, some of them in the pond, many of them bare-breasted, but he only has eyes for his own reflection in the pond. It is such a waste as there is no connection, which is what makes relatedness and enables Heaven on earth. Emotional maturity is the path of ever greater relatedness, love and joy. To get over yourself is to change direction. It is an attitude of joining and the direction is toward another with whom there can be moments of complete joining in love and even transcendent Oneness.

Ask your higher mind to show you where you are so caught up in yourself that others are locked out. Wherever you have built a monument to yourself, let it go because it's blocking your view of life. Heaven on earth means there is a lot less of you and a lot more of Heaven. You are not easily insulted because there is not much of you there to take offense. This allows you to be both available and connected to all around you, with the incumbent happiness that brings. It is said that at the time of enlightenment you become an absolute zero that allows you to experience Oneness. If you want to be happy, get over yourself. If you want to have a successful relationship, get over yourself. Ask to be seen where you are making yourself overly important at work, in your relationship, in the bedroom, by an illness or a problem. When you are miserable, the Idol of Self-Concepts is in your center where you should be. Without you in your center, your life becomes more and more unbalanced and you have to seek outside you for your happiness. Make a choice to head toward joining others with understanding and love.

Chapter 31

Your Emotions are Indicators

The purpose of your emotions is to be indicators. They let you know when you have made a mistake. They let you know that something needs healing. They are indicative of a place where you are off your center and need to be returned to your center if you are to respond to the situation peacefully rather than reactively. An emotion shows where you have a misperception and it means that there is something to correct if you are to respond to the situation with right-minded perception. This opens the door to effective action in the situation so it can be restored to wholeness. This also returns you to innocence because a negative emotion makes you feel bad, and anywhere you feel bad there is guilt. Any place in which you have guilt is a place where you punish yourself. So any place there is a reaction of emotion shows where you have a split mind. The pain, fear and guilt that exist keep the two parts of your mind split. So you want love and you don't want love. You want success and you don't want success. You want health and you don't want health. Of course, you want good things in your life but many of you don't want to go through what it takes to heal the pain and to get where you want to go. You also don't want to lose the independence you got when you lost bonding. Since emotion, ambivalence and independence build the ego, it lobbies you to act in righteous and judgmental ways, with superiority or inferiority, or to be a victim, or to act sacrificially or to remain independent. All these reactions support each other in a vicious circle, along with the pain, guilt and ambivalence already mentioned. Each is part of a pattern of negative emotion from a constellation of negative self-concepts that keeps you stuck.

The purpose of your emotions is to be an indicator, showing you where a whole constellation of self-defeating personalities and emotions exist. They are to let you know where **you** *need to change in order to succeed.* Commit to using such indicators for healing and when the next emotion comes up, go for wholeness.

How you can change using these indicators is by realizing *you* made a mistake and to want to change your mistakes with all your heart. Any place you acknowledge a mistake, your higher mind starts to find a way to change it.

Chapter 32

Self-Pity is an Excuse Not to Change

Feeling sorry for yourself keeps you stuck in the very things about which you are feeling sorry for yourself. Ask yourself how much self-pity you have in regard to yourself? This is not compassion or even empathy. It is an indulgence. You are feeling sorry for yourself. You feel sorry for what has happened to you but you do not really seek to change it or yourself. You are hoping that someone will care and comfort you, but feeling sorry for yourself is a defense that does not really allow contact or comfort. You want it in this case and you don't want it, because if you had it you would change and get on with your life. So, you wallow in self-pity and it is powerful enough to keep you in chronic problems or illnesses.

Self-pity keeps you stuck. It keeps you in the same position, locked in with the same history that you've had. If you go forward, then your history also changes. You look at your life from a higher perspective. You are not held back by it the way you were before. You are evolving once more. Your self-pity, like guilt, is just a way to hide and not deal with your fear. Your fear is healed with love, forgiveness and commitment on your part. These principles turn your gaze away from yourself. So, instead of making life all about you, it brings your attention back to life and others.

Chapter 33

Your Emotions Indicate an Unlearned Lesson

Emotions indicate an unlearned lesson. You might as well learn it now because it will keep repeating until you do. It will keep bringing up the painful emotions, compounded from each situation. Each time there is a new blow-up in a similar but different problem, the situation becomes worse. The lesson has now grown into a trial. In each new situation where no healing occurs you are heading away from life and toward death.

Your ego won't be satisfied until your death, thinking insanely that it will survive it. So it keeps herding you to a place where it appears that there is no way out. Then the ego suggests death as the way out of the terrible, painful emotions and conflicts that you are in. If you don't learn a lesson and it becomes a trial, it can become so painful that you are caught in a pattern of change or die. So you might as well change and you might as well learn the lesson now because if you don't, each new blow up becomes worse than the last.

It's time to change.

Chapter 34

When You Feel Out of Sorts, You Can Change

When you feel out of sorts, take responsibility for what you are experiencing. If you don't take responsibility, nothing will change or you will only change as the tide turns. When you take responsibility, you are empowered to change whenever you choose. You can ask for help. You can center yourself. You can reach out to others. You can go forward. You can help another. These help you change. If you don't like where you are, do something about it. You can forgive. You can let go. You can trust or integrate. You can commit. You can answer another's call for help. You can give or receive. You can bless. You can accept. You can re-bond yourself or you can awaken from the dream you are dreaming. You could share your gifts. You could ask for the truth. You could remember God. All of these work to change your mind and if it doesn't, then all it means is that more healing is needed.

Yet, none of this begins until you take responsibility for your situation. That is the first step and all the other means, such as meditating to regain peace, listening to guidance and the many other forms to transform yourself, begin with taking responsibility.

Chapter 35

Without Healing Yourself, You Lose Your Ability to Feel

Without healing yourself, you lose your feelings. Every problem shows a place where you have lost feeling in your life. It's a place you have lost heart. Your heart is your ability to receive and enjoy. It shows you your purpose and helps you to know truth. Every dark emotion speaks of a place where love has been lost because emotions exist in the place where bonding is meant to be. Every experience of deadness and dissociation shows a place in which you are meant to be feeling good and enjoying yourself.

Take every place you are feeling bad and **commit to your healing**. You could have good feelings instead of problems. You could be feeling good instead of feeling bad. When your commitment to healing is stronger than your fear of the next step, you will naturally go beyond the bad feeling and find the solution to your problem.

Chapter 36

When You Feel Out of Sorts, You Have Stopped Extending

When you feel out of sorts, you have stopped extending yourself. Extending moves you beyond the bad feelings and attendant self-concepts. Judgments and grievances cause problems and encapsulate you in the bad feeling. Extending yourself, especially toward those you have judged and have grievances with, can get you back in the flow and remove the bad feeling you are experiencing. It lifts the anchors of judgment and grievances that hold you back in life.

Extending yourself is what love is. It moves you beyond the boundary that the self-concepts of your ego have placed on you in its desire to build itself in separation and make itself more secure.

Extending yourself builds unity in your own mind and in the world, making one less illusion in both. Extending can let your mind become very quiet and peaceful, beyond any bad feeling you are experiencing at the moment. Extend toward those you love, those who need your help, those around you and those you have used as an excuse not to go forward by your grievances and judgments.

Chapter 37

Don't Be Afraid, Be Happy

Don't be afraid, be happy. In life you have a choice. Sometimes, this choice occurs moment to moment and you have a choice where you want to invest the prodigious power of your mind. Do you want to follow the path of love or fear? Do you want to be afraid or do you want to be happy?

The ego knows that given the choice, you would choose love to the detriment of the ego that relies on the fear that comes from separation. So the ego disguises fear; it sneaks up on you. It tries to keep the fear in the normal, neurotic range of operation.

Let's take worry, for example. Let's say you are worrying about someone. Do you realize that worry, which is society's way of saying, "I care about you", is a form of attack? Do you want to attack that person or do you want to help them? Instead of worrying about them, send your love to them every time you think of them. Have faith in them and their situation.

Emotions are contagious. Research has shown that loneliness is as infectious as the flu. In my work, I have seen evidence of this in regard to all the emotions but especially in regard to fear, depression, anger and guilt.

Yet, love and happiness, confidence and generosity are even more infectious than emotions because these feelings are true. But what is it you want to teach: fear or happiness, guilt or innocence, heaviness or being lighthearted, worry or love? You get to choose.

Do you want to worry about your health, which is self-attack, one of the core dynamics of illness, or do you want to choose to be happy, which, on the other hand, increases health. What are you choosing this minute? Are you choosing to worry about something? Fear shrinks you a couple of sizes smaller. If fear grows, it paralyzes you. Love and happiness create flow. Do you want to choose happiness now? How many times would you have to choose happiness before you could actually experience it? Keep in mind that you always have this choice and that making similar choices time after time creates a direction for you. To follow fear in its direction is to head toward death. To choose happiness brings more and more life and light.

Chapter 38

Choose Love, Not Fear

Choose love, not fear. In any problem we experience there is fear instead of love. A problem shows our split mind. The subconscious part, which is the part least identified with, appears as the obstruction. People who oppose us also reflect the subconscious or unconscious parts of us that have been judged by us. Because of the separation with others, there will also be a split in the more hidden part. Separation generates fear but seems to oppose the part of us that we consciously identify with, and so there is even more fear.

Love heals fear. Love is extending oneself. It is sharing. It is both giving and receiving and it heals the separation that is the ego and that seems to make the world. Our world mirrors our mind and all that we have split off. As we bring love into the world, we heal the separation with joining. This creates a unity and the benignity that comes of harmlessness. Because otherwise, the more fear there is, the more attack there is. Love heals fear and attack is relinquished.

Forgiveness is a form of practical love. It is a realization that no one is to blame and that everything you see is what you think about yourself. In loving anything or anyone, you are loving yourself. In giving to anyone or anything, you are giving to yourself. The more you walk the path of fear, the more you invest in your ego and your mind splits even more. You lose the power that integration brings. You lose the creativity that bridging makes. You lose the joy that love creates.

Today, look out at the world and see yourself mirrored back to you. Choose to love all the pieces of your mind that show themselves to you. If you must begin with forgiveness until you can build up to love, do so but realize that forgiveness extends in the same way love does. It heals the fear and separation that judgment brings. Judgment makes a frightening world just as love makes a peaceful world.

Chapter 39

Your Emotions Deny Divine Presence

Your emotions deny Divine Presence. Every emotion is a complaint that injustice has been done. If you reflect for a moment, you will realize that at the moment the emotion is occurring, you are not thinking about Heaven. This is what the ego wants – to distract you and hide that there is a Heaven and that you can always invoke Divine Presence.

When emotions come up, you can immediately remember and recognize that you have already gone a bit down the ego's path. You have used your emotion to disconnect from Heaven. Once you realize what you have done, you can change your mind and reset your goal. You can invoke Divine Presence once more. This can help you not just endure but transcend any experience you are undergoing. Divine Presence lets you experience something from a much higher perspective, not only removing the pain but using the event itself for you to spring forward and have greater wholeness.

Divine Presence reminds you that grace is always at hand if you open your minds to it. As Thoreau once wrote, "Only that day dawns to which we are awake." You can live a life of grace by letting Heaven interpret everything and do everything through you. If you remember, Divine Presence removes all sacrifice and struggle. It allows you to do what you do with grace and happiness because you are feeling Divine Presence. This connects you not only to Heaven, but to yourself and to others. This opens you to grace-filled and golden moments.

Chapter 40

Your Emotions Knock You Off Your Center

Your emotions knock you off your center. You may have been feeling fine but when emotions arise, they upset you. Emotions may seem to come from outside you but they are always from within. If you want to take a healing stance toward the emotion you are experiencing, then be grateful that the upset has come up because you can tell where you have a pattern that needs to be healed.

Emotions don't actually need a trigger; they simply occur like a mood change. When an emotion comes up you will find that you are off your center. Your center is a place of peace and innocence. It is where love, abundance and joy are generated. But when emotions come up it is easy to get knocked off your center. Even though it seems easy to lose your center, it can be just as easy to return to it. To accomplish this you simply ask your higher mind to return you to your center. This will make things better unless a very big emotion has erupted. Then you can ask to be carried to a second center that is both higher and deeper. By asking again and again, you can be returned to centers that are both higher and deeper. As you ask to be returned to each center, check out how you feel, how the problem looks to you now, how those around you look, how the world looks and how your life looks. Either take yourself to the fourteenth center that is both higher and deeper or continue until the whole scene has turned to light.

This centering exercise is simple and powerful. Let your higher mind do all the work. Your job is simply to witness what has occurred and how you feel. At the end of the exercise, you can ask yourself how long would it have taken you to reach this center if all you had done, and what it had accomplished, had taken place in the normal way without centering. If you become completely centered, even things coming up from within can't bother you or knock you off your center.

Chapter 41

Your Emotions Show Your Attachment

Your emotions show your attachments. When you get upset and experience emotions, it shows that an attachment has been thwarted. As the Buddha said, "All pain comes from attachment". An attachment is a form of false bonding that was made when the attachment was formed. Your ego did this to mimic the bonding you had before, but it is both false and fragile. When an attachment is lost there is sadness and disappointment, and when an attachment is frustrated, there is pain and upset. All the old pain from the lost bonding is hidden there in your attachment which came from the original loss and separation.

An attachment is an illusion, a fantasy made to cover the lost bonding. It is both something we seek and something we hold onto. It is an attempt to get and to take and, because it doesn't deal with the original loss, it is never enough. Your attachments turn you into a parasite depending on a host for your needs. This is a playing out of both sacrifice and dependent roles that will eventually lead to loss as someone in those roles tires and attempts to go independent. This becomes a vicious circle, as independence is also a role. This keeps us blind to the fact that in interdependence there is a level of sharing and love and that roles and taking are not necessary. Where emotions and their ancillary pain spring up, it shows where you have been holding on and trying to take. This puts you in the weakened state of neediness and dependency, which you try to defend with manipulation, control and sometimes sheer bullying. This leads to a bad end, bringing even more pain.

Paradoxically, letting go of your attachments allows your needs to be met. Attachments are used to get your needs met but fail to meet them. When you are empty-handed and unattached, you become attractive and can finally receive because the Universe abhors a vacuum. It takes courage to let go but healing is the only way to free you of self-defeating attachments and letting go is one route to healing. Attachment is not love; it is using and taking. It lacks emotional integrity and so it leads to pain. What lacks integrity is not whole and the split mind has pain between the split off parts. This pain sooner or later comes up and leads to even more pain.

Now, it is time to let go of the pain/attachment, however it shows itself. In a similar fashion, review the past for pain and realize what attachment there is that still needs to be let go of, so you can be freed and restored.

Chapter 42

Displaced Emotions Adversely Affect Your Health

Displaced emotions adversely affect your health. When you do not deal with the conflicts in your mind, the conflict and ensuing emotions cause stress. When they become too strong, they are suppressed or repressed. When what is buried becomes too much, the stress is shunted onto the body. The whole process from conflict to displacement also causes stress and adversely affects both mind and body. As a result, your body, which is a neutral thing, gets punished. It is like having a fight with your spouse, and as a result, kicking the cat. This is not helpful and it distracts you from where the problem really is.

It is your mind that makes your emotions and it is the mistakes of the mind that make you suffer. Illness must be healed at the level that it begins. Otherwise, you are just healing symptoms without the necessary underlying change that frees you. Primordially, under the symptoms are the emotions that led to the illness. At the root of all of these emotions, there is the emotion of fear: fear of change, and fear of the next step. It takes you as long to get over your illness as it takes you to get over your fear. As soon as you have enough confidence for the next stage, the obstacle of illness is no longer needed as an excuse to protect your fear of being inadequate and unable to handle it.

Make a commitment to become aware of emotions and, to stay happy and healthy, heal them as they come up.

Chapter 43

Choose Helping, Not Hindering

Choose helping, not hindering. If you want to build a better life for yourself and a better world, then only helping will do it. Everything you do either helps or hinders. If you do something only for yourself, it is probably not helpful in the long run even for you, although it may seem to be a gain. What favors you only over others is something that makes you become more separated and competitive. This is not helpful in the least. This has the same effect in your mind, giving ascendance to one part and making the parts of your mind more separate and competitive.

Your helpfulness is mutually helpful. It helps others and it helps you. In every situation, ask what you can do to be helpful. Any place you give yourself, any place you are generous, helps the world and it helps you. The world needs you and your helpfulness; it gives you meaning, which is life sustaining. Helping another sets both you and the other in the flow.

One way to help is to bless instead of judge. Your judgment and grievances foster attack and this hinders you grievously and the world a bit. Your ego tries to convince you that the attack you give out is the attack you avoid, but any attack you make outside you, you make inside as well. If you bless another, you bless yourself. If you forgive another, your hidden but projected guilt is dissolved.

When you are emotionally reactive, you are hindering yourself and the situation. When you release emotion without using it as attack, you are healing yourself and helping the situation. Pause from time to time. Look at the people around you. Ask yourself how you can help them. Over the years I have found that if someone around me is in need, especially if I am close to them, then I have the gift they need to be helped or healed. So, ask yourself what the people around you need. The gift is hidden within you and opening and sharing it would have you shine more. Would you be willing to pay that price to help someone you love and who needs you?

In a similar fashion, look at a problem you have. What could you give to the people in the situation, and to the situation itself, that would make a difference? What you give makes a difference. You could see yourself going back through your life and giving to the people in your problems. This helps you release the past that you've dragged into the present. Forgiveness is a gift that always helps in any negative event. It releases you and others from the prison of problems.

Now, ask yourself who in your world needs your help. Forgive them as they show you a part of your mind. Bless them so you bless yourself. Love them so that you, this person, and the world are helped instead of hindered. A problem shows a place where you and the world are hindered. You can render help instead. If another has a problem around you, it shows subconscious and unconscious hindrances within you. Instead of both of you being caught, you can give the soul gift within yourself that would empower and free you both. If you or someone else has a chronic problem, then do this every day.

Chapter 44

If You Are Feeling Bad, Be Helpful

If you are feeling bad, be helpful and you won't feel so bad. Keep being helpful and you won't feel bad at all. Emotions come up. Conflicts occur. Painful situations emerge. Yet, there is an easy way to stay out of the pain in a really transformative way. This is done through helping. Even the most dire pain can be healed in this way. The more take-you-to-your-knees kind of pain it is, the greater the leap forward you experience as you do this exercise. You can also do this with any kind of fear, scarcity or problem in general. Simply imagine the pain between you and the person that most needs your help. See and feel your love and help pass through the pain or problem that surrounds you. As your love goes through the pain, it melts it away and it helps put the person you sent love to and yourself in a flow. It may completely dissolve the pain or problem but, if it is chronic or an issue, then only a layer of it will come off. Still, you can easily heal it layer by layer.

Ask yourself who needs your help. See and feel the blockage between you in whatever form of pain or self-attack it is and then choose to help another rather than attack yourself in this way. Pour your love through the obstruction and into the person who needs you. This will help you both, putting you both in a flow.

Chapter 45

Your Guilt is an Unlearned Lesson

Your guilt is an unlearned lesson. It keeps you stuck. Guilt is a mistake that you have made into a monument. As a mistake you could correct it, but your ego has you enthralled in order to use it for a payoff that does not add one bit to your life. As a matter of fact, it holds you back while it builds your ego. Guilt is what separates you from others and also separates you from love, success and health.

You might examine what hidden purpose the ego has for your guilt to see if it is really worth the self-punishment that all guilt incurs. With this self-attack, you re-enforce the mistake rather than learn the lesson and move on. You live in the past with guilt, reacting to the present as if it was the past. Then you blame others for what you did. There is the glamour of guilt and the attraction of darkness that keeps us snared. But is it really worth more to you than truth, creativity or loving those you love, all of which are shut down with your guilt?

Your guilt is anything you feel bad about. Any emotion from the past that hasn't been released also manufactures guilt to lock it in and go along with it. For instance, if you feel sad, you feel bad and you will punish yourself accordingly. As you learn the lesson and let go, the guilt disappears with the sadness and there is a new beginning. The emotions you carry inside will scar you with emotional grooves or patterns that the guilt locks into your mind. These set beliefs have you perceive the world, relationships and life in a certain fixed, unresponsive and unsuccessful way.

Your guilt is not the truth except to your ego, which has a vested interest in you believing in guilt since it uses guilt to build itself. Guilt means you have misunderstood something and put extra importance on *you* and *your* part in some problem or mistake. Once understood, everything falls into perspective and it no longer obstructs you. You punish neither yourself nor others. You don't withdraw from life but have greater wisdom and confidence because the guilt dissolves as untrue.

Any place you look on the past and it seems dark or painful is a place that is a rich opportunity for healing. As you learn the lesson, it will help you and everyone around you. It will bring greater happiness to you and help uplift those around you.

Chapter 46

Open Yourself to the Treasure Within

Open yourself to the treasure within. If you are feeling bad, it is meant to distract you from some gift within yourself. The bad feeling is actually a form of protection; some kind of insurance the ego has set up so you could be in control and so it could control you. But control is neither confidence nor flow, which is what a gift generates. Flow is not being out of control, which is what the ego tells you would occur if you gave up control.

Even when there is not a negative feeling or a problem, a gift is being offered to you. You have a regular treasure trove inside you. Would you be willing to open the door in your mind to the next gift that is offered you? Would you also be willing to dwell on what gift exists under any bad feeling until it reveals itself to you? By the time it does, you are about ready to receive it. Bad feelings and problems have us dwell on the negativity instead of looking for what is offered within and that is hidden beneath all that is dark or painful. The gift would at the very least be an antidote to the negativity.

Open the door of your mind. Go to the treasure trove. See what you are offered that will enhance your life just as a matter of course. Now do the same with some problem or bad feeling from the past. Be not shy of shining.

Chapter 47

Take Time to Wrap Yourself in Angel Wings

Take time to wrap yourself in *angel wings*. Take a respite from your busy or lonely world. Allow your angel to hold you, wrapping you in their wings to close out the noise and emptiness of the world. Feel yourself held close, comforted beyond all understanding. Let the weariness melt off of you physically and mentally. Let your emotions be healed and feel yourself growing in peace. If you are enmeshed in any trap, feel your angel lifting you up and carrying you forward beyond the travail. The outward circumstances may seem similar when you return from your inner jaunt, but how you look at things will be shifted in an unfolding forward. Any problem is a place where you feel weak and, to some extent, helpless. You feel both ignored and left out while at the same time calling attention to yourself. In the wings of your angel you can let that all come together in integration to a new wholeness so that you feel connected once more to yourself, life, others and Heaven.

Be at peace. Let yourself rest. Be comforted. Let yourself be loved. You are the holy child of God Himself. Let happiness grow in you as you become centered, safe and more whole.

Chapter 48

On the Way to the Big Goal, Set Little Goals

On the way to a big goal, set little goals. A big goal can be overwhelming, the stress of it can sometimes be too much. When you have a giant goal or one that is a lifetime's worth of work, it is much easier to set a small goal so that it is manageable. If you set your next goal with the greater goal in the background, it invites you rather than looms over you, taking your energy and initiative away. If you set another, small but reachable goal just before you reach your little goal then you lose no momentum as you finish your small goal and look for the next. It becomes a seamless movement from goal to goal on the way to your greater goal. From time to time, take some quiet time, hang out with your higher mind to make sure you are on the right track and doing the little goals in the order that would most help you complete the big one.

I learned this when I was working on my doctoral dissertation. I was paralyzed by the amount of work I had to do. I couldn't start, it was too overwhelming but I learned to set a series of small goals on the way to my greater goal and was able to accomplish a prodigious amount of work in a short time. You can handle small goals and step by step they build into great success.

Chapter 49

Be Grateful to Your Team

Be grateful to your team. If you are a success, you have been helped by family, partners, friends and co-workers. Nobody does it on their own for long and lasts to enjoy the success and rewards that come with getting the job done. If you are grateful to your team, they will be grateful to you. A flow is established and a bonding occurs, along with feelings of friendship, cooperation and productivity, even if your functions are at opposite ends of the organizational structure. You weld a team together that has synergy and works smoothly. The same is true of a family as it is of a work unit or a business. Your appreciation of your partner is helpful not just to your partner but to your children also. Your children bask in praise you give not only to them but also to your partner. It helps them in their ability to appreciate both their experience of the family and of themselves. Gratitude creates bonding and the more bonding the less problems. It also allows challenges to be faced with greater confidence and ease than would normally occur.

Chapter 50

You Can't Have It Both Ways

You can't have it both ways. The truth and your way rarely coincide. When they do, you become very successful. You can't cut off your pain and expect to be able to enjoy life. You must go through your pain and have a rebirth of your heart. You can't hold onto a loss and feel your love for someone who is gone. You will either feel the love or the loss. The loss can eclipse the love, or the love will begin melting away the loss leading to a new and better beginning. You cannot expect, demand or manipulate to get what you want and then feel worthy of receiving whatever you got. You can't have it both ways.

When you dissociate pain because you choose to separate, you cannot expect to heal yourself because the dissociation heads you away from healing and into denial and defensiveness. It hides what needs healing.

You can't expect to have confidence and a split mind because each part of your mind has a different goal. You can't have it both ways. If you are in a conflict it will generate fear and that stops you from going forward. The key is to get your split mind back together. Wherever your mind is split is a place you have lost bonding, but it is more true to say it is a place you have given up bonding. Where you have given up bonding you made a 'bad guy', someone you blame for the broken bonding. Your fear and blame keeps your mind split. Pain, guilt and fear are there to keep splits apart. Healing removes the negative emotion and brings the splits together in new wholeness. This also removes the blame. As you forgive someone, you remove your hidden guilt. You can't have blame and be innocent; it doesn't work both ways.

You can't have dissociated independence and feel free, as you are always running from neediness, commitment and anything that reminds you of your unhappy past. Independence is a role and is dissociated and reactive. It compensates for need, fear and guilt and it is always tied to the roles of victim and sacrifice. Likewise, you cannot have the victim role and be strong and powerful. You cannot have the sacrifice role and have the equality that brings partnership and fosters love. You can't have a role and have success or intimacy because roles are dissociative and block receiving and reward. You can't have happiness and be right. Being right is winning in a competitive way and this separates you. Being right is also a compensation for guilt that doesn't want you to be happy, as being happy shows the extent you are bonded. You can't have it both ways; you can't be loving and separate because love is joining. You can't be loving and fearful because they are opposites. You can't believe in good and evil and believe that you are good. This is because the system itself promotes that you have both good and evil within you, in spite of how you may compensate by acting religious, good, helpful, righteous, judgmental or blaming. The guilt may be hidden but it still affects you by not allowing you to receive and punishing you.

You can't wish something on others and expect to escape it yourself. You can't have it both ways, which is why all healing has to do with integration and bringing things into a new wholeness. When your mind has a new level of integrity, whatever negativity there was is added to a positive wholeness. Both ways come together and it is only in wholeness that you allow yourself to receive and have what you want. One easy way is to hand the negativity over for integration by your higher mind whose job it is to correct mistakes. Choose that all the levels of conflict be integrated as sometimes conflict goes down many levels.

Chapter 51

Your Ambivalence is Killing You

Your ambivalence is killing you. It is your split mind that stops you from going forward. If you are not going toward life then you are going toward death. Your change is your cure but a split mind generates a fear of change. If you are not changing, you are getting old, staying stuck and dying. Your ambivalence keeps you fence-sitting and human anatomy is not made for fence-sitting. It is time to bring the splits in your mind together. Even to bring two negatives or two positives together creates new empowering wholeness. This brings peace and peace opens your mind to inspiration, guidance and a responsive centeredness. Choosing to have a split integrated is an easy form of integration. Commitment, giving yourself wholly to something, also brings together two splits from the past.

Commit to wholeness. Commit to it every day. It will save you a lot of pain and it will easily transform a lot of self-defeating patterns.

Now is the time to give up all roles, compensations, dualities, opposing feelings, dilemmas, heartbreaks and victimizations as they are evidence of your split mind. Commit instead to the true change that restores life. Each commitment takes you another step forward in life, generating change.

Chapter 52

Your Ambivalence Keeps You in Scarcity

Your ambivalence keeps you in scarcity. Your ambivalence keeps you from receiving because you want something and you don't want it. Even if your conscious mind thinks it wants something completely, if you wanted it fully, you would have it.

All scarcity comes down to this, you want something and you don't want it and your not wanting it is stronger. Of course, you hide this part from yourself, which is why we have a subconscious mind to relegate such parts to.

You know you want something but you could ask yourself these questions to find some of the subconscious reasons you don't want it. If you were to heal any of these dynamics well you would dissolve the scarcity.

- What purpose does it serve you not to have what you think you want?
- What are you afraid would happen if you got what you wanted?
- What are you afraid you would lose if you got what you wanted?
- What does not having what you want allow you to do?
- What guilt are you paying off by not having what you want?
- What don't you have to do by not having what you want?
- What are you getting to prove by not having what you want?
- Who are you trying to defeat by not getting what you want?
- What are you attacking yourself for by not having what you want?

- What excuse does not having what you want give you?
- Besides yourself, who are you getting revenge on to not have what you want?
- What are you trying to control yourself about by not having what you want?
- Who else are you trying to control by not having what you want and about what?
- How does this scarcity get you attention and specialness?
- By not having what you want, what else are you trying to get and from whom?
- What is the soul gift within yourself you are denying by this scarcity?
- What aspect of your purpose are you running from by this scarcity?
- What does this scarcity allow you to hide from?

All of these questions have answers and knowing these answers is more than halfway to achieving what you want. Your choice to release these mistakes allows a better way. Begin now.

Chapter 53

You Will Not Escape What You Do

Everything you do to another will be done to you. Let us say you broke bonding with your parents because it looked like they did something to you, or didn't do something for you, or it looked like they didn't love you. By breaking that bonding and separating, you will have people do the same to you because you will have set up a pattern of heartbreak, loss, attack and self-attack.

If you have a partner who doesn't love you enough, it goes back to a place *where you believed that you were unloving.* The present situation is the result. Naturally this has been hidden away in your subconscious but all you need do is guess intuitively and trust the first thing that pops into your mind.

When something dark, painful or negative happens to you, ask yourself:

"If I were to know the root of something I did that caused this, it began for me at the age of..."

"And what I did that set this pattern in motion was that I..."

See yourself back there and, this time, choose peace and greater bonding. Choose not to run and hide. Choose to give yourself. Receive Heaven's gift and the soul gift you brought in, so no negative pattern would begin. Share yourself and your gifts. Embrace the purpose and destiny you ran from. These are positive choices to have things progress in the most positive way. As this hidden past that you have been carrying around dissolves, so will your present situation ameliorate and once again there will be receiving, ease and flow.

Chapter 54

You Will Not Escape What You Wish on Others

The mind is all inclusive. In the place that it exists out of time in Oneness, it is aware of Oneness and joy but most of us put our focus on a lower level of consciousness. At the subconscious or interpersonal level, we reap what we sow and what goes around comes around, as the sayings go. At the unconscious level of the mind, the world is our mirror. Everything we try to do to anyone in the mirror is what we are doing to ourselves and if we break the mirror by our attack, well, that's just a lot of bad luck.

I first discovered this when I began working with people who felt cursed in their lives. Curses are relatively easy to remove. However, at times this can be a bit delicate because if someone has truly been cursed by a master, the curse may have been booby-trapped against anyone blithely attempting to remove it. The people who had symptoms of being cursed were people who were unconsciously cursing others. They did not realize that every time they cursed another, part of them withered from the curses they gave themselves as well.

When you judge or attack others, you judge and attack yourself. The ego loves this because it builds itself not only through judgment and attack but also through self-judgment and self-attack. This is the very foundation of the ego beyond which, it tells you, is your death. But beyond this level of attack is joy, which is the ego's death.

The ego is quite invested in your remaining caught in the belief that you need such mistaken and painful wishes toward others. It has convinced you that if you attack others you will escape attack, but this is a mistake. You don't escape what you wish or do to others.

Chapter 55

Let Sex Be a Joining

Let sex be a joining. Anything less than this and you cheat yourself. Sex is many things. At its worst it becomes a weapon or a form of politics to dominate or abase oneself. This is a great mistake as sex can be not just a vehicle of love, but also an agent of transformation, healing and comfort. For that to occur, there must be joining. That means that it goes beyond the physical. To keep it on the physical plane only is just like changing the oil in the car. It's no big deal. But when there is joining, there is meaning. Love occurs. You are moved forward. If you are in a fight or there is deadness or some other problem, you are moved beyond it to a new step.

Set your intention that all of your sex be a way to join your hearts and your minds. Then your relationship and sex life will keep growing to even greater wholeness.

Chapter 56

Let Sex Be a Welcoming

Let sex be a welcoming. Let yourself welcome your partner into you fully. Open your heart. Open your mind. Receiving is a form of love. Welcoming is a form of love. When joining occurs at this level, the dream of the world can fall away and Oneness can be experienced. Let go of grievances. Cancel your reservations. Give up worry. Throw away considerations. Let yourself be guided by the spirit of love. Take down the walls of your ego and let your partner in. Invite them into your innermost sanctuary. Let your joining be an offering on the altar of your heart-mind. To the extent that you welcome another, you welcome Heaven. Let your partner be safe and healed and whole in the sanctuary of your mind. Welcome Heaven in to restore your partner and give whatever they need to heal them. If you don't have what they need, Heaven will give it to you for them if you ask. Then you simply receive it and share it with them. Welcome the gifts Heaven has for you and your partner as you make love.

Chapter 57

Give Up Your Grievances

Give up your grievances. They're killing you. There is no problem that does not have a grievance as one of its core roots. Let go of the grievance and you let go of the problem. There is no illness or scarcity that doesn't have a grievance at its root. While we are righteous about the grievances we hold, it blinds us to the fact that our grievances hide our guilt. Both grievances and guilt are ways that the ego builds itself at our expense. There is no guilt that we do not punish ourselves for and there is no grievance that we do not try to punish another for. Again, this self-attack and attack is the very foundation of the ego.

To be free, happy and healthy, make it a life-long policy to let go of grievances. Every day examine your problems and ask who you might have a grievance with that keeps this problem going. Then choose to let it go and in its place have the confidence and success of the next step.

Look at any emotions that you have, because any place of upset is the place of a grievance. Let it go. Examine your life past and present, especially looking for old painful stories and for anyone you feel less than loving toward. For their sake, for your sake, for the sake of those you love and for Heaven's sake, let go of your grievances.

Chapter 58

Give Up Your Life of Hard Labor

Take a good look at your life. Do you have a life of hard labor? Since we write our scripts and life stories, what is the purpose of writing a life of hard labor for yourself? Research shows that industry and hard work are important for getting started and getting a good foundation when you are beginning a new project. As a matter of fact, for someone to become an expert in their field, such application is called for. Give yourself continually to your field of work for five to ten years and you begin to make connections that improve your profession. You become a pioneer and even a visionary to find a new and better way but it really takes commitment. Then the rewards follow.

But at a certain point, it is not about hard work. It is about surrender, which means letting go of attachments, integrating opposites and healing shadows. In the joining that brings surrender, the power struggle and deadness fostered by competition are healed. After learning about applying yourself, the next stage is about learning to partner with others, which helps you integrate disparate parts of your own mind. The next major stage of learning is about receiving.

In the first level of life, we learn about giving and being industrious. This can work very well when it is an act of giving. Then, at the next level when you are learning surrender, you learn to achieve the balance of your masculine and feminine sides so that partnership is achieved. At the next level of evolution, the lesson focuses on greater balance, the ascendency of receiving and the feminine side. This is what leaps us forward and allows us to receive grace and miracles as we evolve spiritually.

I have found that some people have condemned themselves to a life of hard labor because of guilt or feelings of failure. Others have condemned themselves to a life of hard labor because they are afraid they are not good enough. Others have a fear of intimacy, success, their giftedness or their purpose and so they push themselves at work to avoid goals they seemingly want.

Ask yourself how many selves you have condemned to a life of hard labor.

What were they condemned for? Can you see that this works against your ostensible goals of greater love and success because these selves can't receive. Would you commute their sentences and see them melting back into you, bringing new peace and greater flow and confidence for success?

Chapter 59

Commute Your Sentence

One of the things I found over the years as I worked with the thousands of personalities that people have, is that a personality cannot receive. This is so even though it is a self-concept of separation with its own belief system and goals as to what it thinks would make you happy. It is like wearing a giant condom. Self-concepts rob you of flow, enjoyment and the contact that brings success.

Personalities can be toxic and negative but they can also be positive. The problem with the positive ones is that it does positive, even gifted, action but you receive no reward for this. As personalities cannot receive, the more self-concepts you have, the more self-conscious you are. This prevents you from hearing the calls for help. Responding to calls for help is one of the most fulfilling things you can do. When you are stopped, not in the flow or have a problem, you could simply ask yourself who needs your help and imagine this pushing through the self-attack or whatever is holding you up. This then 'pops' the self-concept and there is flow once more. The ego doesn't want you to be in a flow so it typically sends another self-concept to stop you. It is common to have many self-concepts that are the same. It is the same with a problem in that there might be many more than one layer to it. Simply repeat the exercise to heal the next attack or the next layer. Ask who else needs your help and send love or blessings through the problem or self-concept.

I have found in the last decade that some personalities have been arrested. This stops your development and the possibility of letting go or integration, either of which would heal the split off personalities.

- How many arrested personalities do you have in your life?
- What impact are these having in your life?
- Would you be willing to melt these down to their pure energy and let them be integrated back into you, to create a new level of wholeness?
- How many selves do you have that are imprisoned?
- What impact is this having on your life?
- Would you be willing to have these selves melt down to their pure energy and then be integrated back into you, to give you a new level of confidence?
- How many selves do you have in solitary confinement?
- What impact is this having in your life?
- Would you imagine these all melting down to their pure energy so they can be integrated for a new level of intimacy in your life?
- How many selves do you have that are on death row?
- What impact is this having on your life?
- Would you be willing to melt these back into you to increase your ability to receive?
- How many selves do you have that have died?
- What parts of your body are they buried in?
- What effect is this having on your health and on your life?
- Would you imagine these melting down to their pure energy and thereby increasing the flow in your life?
- How many parts of your body have been wounded?
- What effect are these having on your life?
- Would you be willing to melt down the wounded selves and return this energy to restore these parts of your body?
- How many unconscious selves do you have from shocking and traumatic events?
- How many unconscious selves do you have from using up all your psychic, mental and emotional energy to try to save someone or a situation?
- What effect is this having on your life?
- Would you be willing to blow the sacred breath of life to awaken these selves and melt them into wholeness so you have more victories in your life?
- How many selves do you have that are on skid-row as homeless people or bag-ladies?
- What effect is this having in your life?

- Would you be willing to melt these selves down to greater wholeness so you are much more rewarded in your life?
- How many selves do you have that are psychotic?
- What effect are these having in your life?
- Would you melt these personalities back into you so that you have greater inspiration in your life?
- How many neurotic selves do you have inside?
- What effect are these having in your life?
- How many selves do you have that are possessed?
- Would you call in the angels to free you and send the ghosts, entities, etc. back to the light while melting your selves back to wholeness?
- Would you be willing to melt these back into you to increase your loving and creative energy?

Doing these exercises can create a much greater capacity of will, innocence, strength and power. This allows more loving energy and the ability to receive and experience greater joy in your life.

Chapter 60

Cancel Your Reservations

Cancel your reservations. Cast aside your doubts. Let go of your considerations. Put your worries in Heaven's Hands. They are all meant to stop you from going forward. There is no problem that does not have fear of the next step as a key dynamic.

Reservations, doubt and consideration stop you from finding the truth. The truth gives you direction, makes things easy and sets you free.

Become aware of which of these traps are holding you back and instead commit to the next step. Every day and every time you have some doubt, reservation or worry come into your mind, ask, choose, pray and give yourself fully so that the direction you want to go in becomes clear to you. No matter what, you want to go in the direction of the truth so that you do not waste your time and your life. The truth has a way of clarifying things so that what is untrue falls away without effort and suffering is lessened.

All of your reservations, considerations and doubts keep you wasting time fence-sitting and human anatomy was not made for fence-sitting.

Do not be stopped by the last trap of the ego before partnership. Step up through commitment and find what's true.

Chapter 61

Be Mindful

Be mindful. Mindfulness is the awareness that expands your consciousness, until you transcend consciousness for Awareness. As your consciousness expands on the way to Awareness, you feel even more joyful because you see more and more of the interconnectedness of all things.

Being mindful means you don't get caught in temptation, the dark glamour of the victim or the attraction of guilt. You don't make bad guys to hide your own guilt and fear about not stepping up. You don't indulge in self-attack, knowing it always comes when there is someone in need of your help. To be mindful is to hear the calls for help as well as to be aware of your own feelings and motivations. Because you are not using guilt or judgment against yourself and others, it is easy to understand and embrace the deeper parts of your mind, as well as those who are in need. Being mindful creates flow so whenever you are out of the flow, engage in mindfulness once more.

Being mindful brings you back to the present and this centers you. You aren't caught in the bad feelings of the past or fear of the future. Peace is in the present and from peace there is joy, love, health and abundance. Commit to mindfulness. The expanded awareness makes you high and if there is greater peace and mindfulness, we open to vision. Greater mindfulness brings the quiet mind of mastery that blesses the earth with all it receives.

Chapter 62

Be Mindless

Be mindless. The more mindless you are, the more ecstatic you are. People meditate for years to become peaceful enough to be mindless. In mindlessness, the tens of thousands of self-concepts have melted away. What is left in their place is the profound joy that leads to love, abundance and transcendence. This is the quiet mind where there is a portal to timelessness.

All of your self-concepts give you jobs. Each self-concept tells you that all you need do is follow what is necessary to complete *its* task, rather than that of all the others. This leads to competition and conflict, which gives us stress and generates fear.

To be mindless is to have a clear mind. It means there's less of you and more of Heaven. You are aligned with Heaven instead of your ego. You can achieve the state that opens to the void that Buddha achieved, in which there is bliss and the awareness that it was our mind that made the world. From the mindlessness you can reach a place where you experience the Great Rays, the experience of God.

Being mindless can be achieved by meditation or some forms of yoga. But it can also be achieved by giving totally, as best you can, to everyone and everything. In much the same way, if you forgive everyone and everything, especially the ones you are having trouble with, it can lead to vision, mastery and mindlessness.

Profound acceptance, letting go and trust can also bring this about. Finally, loving everyone and everything has this same effect. It can also bring about miracles, which leap you and others forward. Your mind gets quieter in mindlessness and you hear Divine inspiration lifting you up. Mastery mind is the quiet mind. In mindlessness, there are answers, joy, peace, humor, intuition and general happiness. Mindlessness occurs the more centered we become. The more there is nowhere to go and nothing necessarily to do, the more you open to the part of your mind that leads to the Mind of God.

Chapter 63

When You Don't Like What You See, Change Your Mind

When you don't like what you see, change your mind. Perception is a matter of choice. What you see comes from your beliefs and you are responsible for what you believe. You are also responsible for what you see. There is a payoff for you in seeing what you see. Those giving love, see love. Those attracted to guilt, see symbols of guilt. You see what you want to see. You see what has interest to you, much like a husband and wife looking in a department store window with the wife looking at the dress and the husband looking at the golf clubs.

Perception can be changed to something truer and more favorable. To do this you must first take responsibility for what you see. Once you do that, if it's of interest, you can ask yourself the purpose you have for seeing such a scene.

- What does it allow you to do?
- What excuse does it give you?
- Does it make someone else wrong to hide your own guilt?
- What do you get to be right about now as a result of this?
- What does this prove to you?
- Does it lead toward love or toward fear?
- What gift does this scene hide?

These are just a few questions that you can ask yourself.

Next, ask if the scene has changed for you, and then apply the power of choice. Here are a couple of statements from or inspired by *A Course in Miracles* designed to do just that:

- I could have peace instead of this.

- I want to see this scene truly. I will not use this scene as a sign of sin, destruction and death. I will not use this scene as an obstruction to peace but as a means to it.

  Keep giving energetically to the scene.
  Keep forgiving the scene and the people in it.
  Pour your trust into everything turning out beautifully.
  Give yourself to everyone in the situation and the situation itself.
  Ask for grace to pour through you into your perception.
  Repeat these exercises time and again until the situation is not only benign but joyful.

Chapter 64

Your Emotions Are Your Choice

Your emotions are your choice. The experiences that give rise to your emotions are your choice. You chose emotions and dark experiences at the deepest level to run from yourself and your greatness. You could shine instead; you could embrace your sacred promise to help the world and those you came to help.

You can go back through your life and examine the big emotions and mishaps in your life.

What was it you were trying to get?

What was it that you were running from?

Can you accept that these choices were a mistake?

Knowing what you know now, what would you choose instead?

See yourself making that choice back there. How do things turn out now?

How is your life different as a result of that choice?

What soul gift awaits you if you make that choice, instead of breaking bonding, going down the path of the ego and paying the pound of pain to be more independent?

Would you also receive Heaven's gift instead of the ego's path of pain?

Would you embrace the purpose that you promised you would do instead?

Would you instead embrace the destiny of who you came to be, with all of its grandeur of the Golden Life Story that you turned away from?

Would you give up this excuse not to show up, that is full of pain and dark dreams?

If you take responsibility and see how you set up the whole event, can you see how, as your excuse, you made a scapegoat of the very person that you were meant to help?

Emotional Maturity Series

Your emotions are your choice and you could have chosen to open your soul gifts and lovingly share them with the person who became your villain. You had to wound yourself as you attacked them. Can you instead open your compassion for yourself and them? Can you receive your gifts and Heaven's, and embrace your purpose and destiny?

Next when you are tempted to react emotionally, remember what you are avoiding and choose again. You could have peace instead. You could have gifts, Heaven's Presence and grace, as well as a new aspect of your purpose and destiny.

118

Chapter 65

Don't Be Afraid of the Dark

Don't be afraid of the dark. According to quantum physicists, what underlies all reality is light. It is beyond every appearance. Mystics would say that this light is spirit, love, Oneness, and God, and that all else is the illusion.

Darkness comes from separation and judgment. It is really a dream of breaking apart. The illusion occurs as bonding is lost. The more judgment and separation that seem to occur, the more darkness there is. With the darkness comes dualism, pain, need, fear, resistance, loss, feelings of abandonment and guilt. It appears real. Yet, it is the dream that quantum physicists say began with choice. This is also stated in *A Course in Miracles* and echoed in Psychology of Vision.

Darkness is the illusion and thus it can be changed. This is what healing is: bringing more wholeness and light into a picture. This is why when a healer brings enough light from their being, any problem can be resolved. At its root, a problem is simply the separation that leads to the dark but the light is more essential. It is important to realize that you are the light and the light is in you, as you. All darkness will eventually fall away and the truth will prevail. It will take time to bring the light fully to this world of illusion. Writings around *A Course in Miracles* speak of how it took millions of years to get to this place of darkness and it may take as many or even more years to get back to a place of pure light. It is important not to be afraid of the dark because it is the light that is the truth of the matter. Don't be bullied by an illusion but invoke the light instead.

The darkness disappears when someone turns on a light. Every time there is pain or a problem, commit to the truth. Ask for the light. Want the truth with all your heart. Even if you were to face the darkness of the astral world with its demons, you could only be frightened if you forgot Who walked beside you. We all have beings of light to help and protect us.

The world mirrors your mind and the darkness you see outside you is simply the projection of the darkness that is within you, which comes from lost bonding. You need not be afraid of your own mind though the ego throws fear and guilt at you to try to stop you. Even ancient fragments of the ego, also known as demons and which seem to have a mind of their own, can all be brought back to the light through your light and the power of the light beings who walk beside you. There is no place the light is not.

Chapter 66

Receive What Heaven Wants to Give You

Receive what Heaven wants to give you because Heaven wants to give you everything. It is the nature of Heaven. If you have a problem, you could spend time quietly, opening yourself to what Heaven wants to give to you. Yet, it is not just in a problem situation that Heaven wants to give to you but in every situation. Heaven loves you totally and knows that you deserve it all. On the other hand, your ego has made up fear and guilt and every manner of negativity to hold you back, as it depends for its maintenance on you being stuck or reactive.

Heaven wants to make your way easy. Heaven wants you to find your way Home. Heaven wants Heaven on earth for you. Heaven knows your innocence and worth despite what your ego tells you. Heaven just wants you to open the door and allow it to give to you, ending some of the separation that holds you back from Heaven and from your brothers and sisters here on earth. Your life could be graceful. You could have peace and abundance instead of the life that you made. Today and every day, spend time opening to all the gifts that Heaven wants to give you for no other good reason than that you are God's beloved child.

Chapter 67

Giving Wholeheartedly Makes You Happy

Giving wholeheartedly makes you happy. It gives meaning to whatever you do, opens doors that were previously closed, and generates ease. Wholehearted giving is a form of love that allows you to receive wholeheartedly. It re-bonds you and creates flow and mutuality with whomever and whatever you give to. Wholeheartedness graduates you to the next stage. If you are not doing well, you improve because resistance dissolves. With wholehearted giving, you either become centered emotionally in what you are doing or centered emotionally with those around you. Other possibilities arising from wholehearted giving are that the situation changes in such a way that you experience yourself in a much better position, or that your partner or the situation improves as a result. It can even be that your situation or your partner fall away because they are not true and another position or partner that is true comes to you so a new level can begin. But if this change occurs, there is no pain or loss, simply a feeling that it was the right thing to happen. Then new developments occur. Developments come to you that would not otherwise have been available.

Giving wholeheartedly helps you be your best self and this makes you feel good about yourself in spite of what is going on. Giving wholeheartedly over a few months begins to expand your mind so that your intuition, timing and luck grow. If you persevere and give yourself fully, it becomes a way of life, so that levels of creativity, confidence, psychic ability, artistic or healing gifts become natural. You open up both vision and the ability to bring the positive future into the present.

If you keep going in this direction, the shamanic mind develops with its ability to transcend the natural laws.

Choosing to give yourself fully empowers you. It expands the capacity of your mind as well as your luck because you are so in the flow.

If you are in a job or a relationship and you are not giving yourself 100%, you are cheating yourself. Whatever and whoever, you fully give yourself to become better. It makes you better and it gives you deeper enjoyment and more creativity in your life.

Chapter 68

When You're Feeling Bad, Commit to the Next Step

When you are feeling bad, commit to the next step. Feeling bad means you are caught in a conflict. It could even mean that two parts of your mind are on their way to integration, and the emotions that keep them apart are now being jammed together enough to 'come up'. Committing to the next step takes you out of the present conflict. You may still be experiencing some of the emotions but at a more secondary level and not so much 'in your face'. Commit again and they become even less. Commit again and they become 'no big thing'. Commit again and again and they dissolve completely, though it may be that your choosing the step with all your heart is all you need to move through the conflict altogether. Sometimes you will face the same emotions further down the road but at a whole new level, and having healed them once the second time is not as big.

If you experience these bad feelings at a lighter level, it means that you are moving through them. If it is much stronger, it means that you have opened up a layer of unconscious emotions and typically, after you have committed once or twice more, those particular emotions abate. Only in the rarest cases will you go deeper into the last bastion of defense. This is where the ego throws everything at us to prevent us aligning our will with Heaven's and as a result winning back the chunks of our primordial mind that have been split off. The emotions at this level can show themselves as misery, devastation, anguish, agony, bad attitude, willfulness, recalcitrance and passive-aggression. There may also be astral attack, but ultimately it is all our authority conflict and acting out the rebel with God. This stage can even extend into a 'Dark Night of the Soul' or to the final '*The Dark Night of the Soul*' before we regain the realization of Oneness.

While these last levels are more rare, they are sometimes attached to chronic problems where a person consciously wants it to get better but at an unconscious level has contracts with the ego and with death. Commitment to the next step, wanting the next stage with your whole heart, keeps you turned toward the light. That and your wholehearted desire will bring you to a unity in your mind and then to union and finally Oneness, all the time bringing you back your power, your love, and more and more grace in your life.

So, whenever you are feeling bad, or even feeling good, commit to the next step.

Chapter 69

When You Are Happy, You Give Wholeheartedly

When you are happy, you give wholeheartedly. Happiness is a sign of love and when you feel love, you naturally give all of yourself. Love, happiness and giving yourself wholeheartedly create an ascending spiral of consciousness that is the natural antidote to dilemmas and vicious circles, which spiral downwards.

Any problem shows a place where we are not happy and not giving ourselves fully. It is a place that lacks love in some way. It is a place where you could discover where you are not giving yourself 100% and could change your mind. If you were happy, this would naturally happen. You would want to give yourself fully. Unhappiness points to a place where you are not giving yourself fully. If you expect the outside situation to make you happy, you may wait a long time. Equally, if you are happy because you are dependent on how things are outside you, how you feel could change as the outside situation changes.

Enjoy when outside circumstances make you happy. Situations like that come and go. But your happiness need not depend on your outer circumstances. You can choose to be happy. Whenever there is a negative situation, remember that the alternative is happiness and you can choose it.

"I could have happiness instead of this" could be your mantra. Happiness comes from loving yourself. Any place you do not love yourself, you won't love those around you and you won't give yourself 100% so that you could feel problem free.

Take responsibility for your happiness. When you have it, you give yourself fully and success grows. If you are not happy, you are complaining about someone and something while ignoring the gift within that would transform the problem. It would help others and make you happy to realize your gift and share it. Be happy and as you give yourself fully, you make others happy because you have added to the increase. You have also added to everyone's flow and innocence, which are key ingredients in happiness.

Chapter 70

Expectations are the Bane of Success

Your expectations are your demands, and your demands are off-putting even to you. You not only make demands on others, you make the same ones on yourself. Or you will make them first on yourself and then on others. What you do to others, you will do to yourself and vice versa. Expectations are compensations for our needs, and our needs and demands push people away; they resist when you attempt to get or take from them. The need/demand/expectation also sets up the split mind so that expectation demands to have the need met, but that is secondary to remaining independent.

Expectations also compensate for feelings of inadequacy and, at this level, you resist having what you seemingly want, because if you got it, you wouldn't know what to do with it because you feel inadequate.

Expectations push too much. They try to take and can't receive. They try too hard for success. At this stage you live a hidden life of fantasy about how your need should be met. But even if your fantasy would be realized, it wouldn't meet the need. The purpose of a need is for it to be met and not be met at the same time. To meet a need you must come from a single-minded intention of joining and receiving instead of the split mind of expectations and need, wanting to receive and wanting to be independent. The extent of your frustration and disappointment in life is the extent of your expectations. You can't force life or people into your picture of how things should be. It won't please them or satisfy you.

Your expectations are based on attachments and it is your attachments that lead to pain and scarcity. As you let go of your expectations, the attachments and needs are let go of also and you progress. Having emptied yourself of expectations, you can now receive and, by releasing stress and establishing flow, this will make all the difference in your life.

Chapter 71

Every Problem Shows a Fear of Change

Every problem shows a fear of change. This delays you until you have the courage to say "Yes" to the inevitability of change. You could keep delaying but it would become destructive. You would turn away from life instead of saying "Yes" to it. When you change you don't become something different, you become more yourself. Unless, of course, you are running away from yourself, then you set up destruction. What you fear you resist and a problem is your resistance coming back at you. Your willingness cuts through fear. You have fear of something negative occurring but that only hides the fear of your purpose and greatness.

Your commitment to change keeps you young because you are willing to learn and keep moving forward. You become more flexible and able to bend rather than break. You grow in confidence as you keep moving forward. You become more whole as you keep moving forward.

Choose to change. It will make all the difference in your life. Your life may be good but it could get better. And if it is not good, you are definitely the one that needs to change. If you don't see that your change is your cure, then you are in trouble and probably lost in misery, complaints and blame, which will only make it worse. Decide for change. Choose to change. Commit to change. It is for your own good.

Chapter 72

When Something is Missing in Your Life, You're Not Bringing It

When something in your life is missing, it is because you are not bringing it. This may sound crazy to someone who feels bankrupt, but bankruptcy represents a series of bad decisions that were made, all leading to a place of feeling powerless. This does not take away from the core issue – that what you are seeking is inside of you. It is really inside you, but you have displaced what is missing under pain and even misery. Underneath those emotions there is a layer of blame and grievance. Next comes a layer of guilt and failure. Then comes a level of fear of the gift that was in you all the time. Then comes the gift itself. Were you to heal the misery, anger, guilt or fear completely, you would heal enough to realize you have the very thing inside you that you have been seeking for outside you. It's like having a mansion in the desert set for a feast, but all the while running out to look for food and water.

Bring to your relationships what you are seeking outside yourself. No longer seek outside; it is inside. This is where *being* is having. I've had many marriage partners complain they weren't getting enough sex. But when they gave up trying to take from their partner to fulfill their needs and brought equality and sexual energy, they had more than enough sex.

What's missing in your life? What have you been complaining about? That shows something that you are not giving. Now, imagine going to the door in your mind that houses the very thing that you need. Open that door. Embrace that gift energetically and let it fill you. Then, with the energy of the gift, touch the problem that was trying to keep you from that door. This will dissipate what's holding you back and the scarcity itself. The obstacle's only purpose was to stop you and now that is gone. As you dissolve a defense and embrace a gift there is more natural flow in your life, as well as the giving and receiving of what was missing in your life.

Chapter 73

To Be Safe, Be Harmless

You know that you reap what you sow. This is opposite to the ego's message that the attack you make on others allows you to escape from attack. But this is not how the mind works. Whatever you do to others, you do to yourself. Whatever you wish on another, you wish on yourself. This is why one of the principles of mastery is to be harmless. There is a quote from *A Course in Miracles* that goes: "In defenselessness, your safety lies."

The ego tells you to make defense after defense to protect yourself. But a defense brings about the very thing it is meant to prevent. You defend old pain and old pain becomes both victim and attacker. Your attack calls in more attack and the pain of being a victim is part of a pattern that will branch out, generating more victim situations until it is healed.

What you defend against gets attacked. The ego uses this to compound the pain, have you withdraw further and build bigger defenses, thus expanding itself. Your higher mind, on the other hand, uses whatever comes up to learn and heal. This melts away your defenses leaving you open, but not weak and vulnerable as the ego tells you. You become more confident and less insecure as you remove your defenses. You finally learn the painful, unlearned lesson you had inside. You recognize it for what it is and heal it. As a result, you leap forward.

As a defense is set up, it attacks you or others. If someone goes to breach your defenses, you make them wrong for hurting you. You become so defended that only the greatest adept can penetrate your defenses without setting off a trip wire. You use your wounds for a purpose. They become your most precious commodity. You are more married to your pain than to your partner. Your pain becomes your best excuse.

You have a story about how you were an innocent victim and how those around you did you wrong. You project your guilt and forget that you are the one writing the story of your life. At the deepest levels, you assigned everyone the roles they played in your script.

Consciously, it is just the opposite. All your pain was the result of someone infringing on you and harming you. But this was just the excuse you needed to run from who you really are. You are afraid of your love and greatness. You are afraid of purpose, which was what you came to contribute. Your purpose is your sacred promise. In giving it you know yourself and can embrace your destiny of living the Golden Life on the way to realizing yourself as a joyful spirit, safe and whole with no need to defend yourself. Until that point, you either move toward greater defensiveness or you move toward partnership. Defensiveness infringes on others and sets up an inability to receive, leading you to make others the object of exploitation. However, in partnership there is a natural giving and receiving in mutuality.

Choose to be open. Welcome the feedback life has for you. Forgive all you see in the mirror that the world constantly provides for you. Be compassionate. What you see is all you. It is your belief system about yourself. Do not defend yourself. It sets up greater conflict than the one already inside that led to this energy and force coming toward you. In truth, the force is you. If you accept and even welcome what comes toward you, the pain you have inside that you are afraid to experience dissolves easily into birth. This is the easiest possible way to leap forward and even to pass the great shamanic and mastery level tests of your life that you didn't pass before. When you don't pass a shamanic level test, it feels as if your heart is getting ripped out. If you don't pass a mastery level test you feel as if your world has collapsed and crushed you. It is time to give up your defenses so they don't victimize others. It is time to give up your victim pain that is really revenge. It is time to be harmless and feel the carefreeness that comes of safety.

Chapter 74

Fear of What You Want

You would have everything you wanted in life if you were not frightened to have it. Your need for it proves your fear of it, as these two dynamics are different halves of the same whole. When you have a need, if you are aware, you notice you have a fear that your need won't be met. However, if you allowed yourself to see into your subconscious, then you would realize that you are not only afraid to not have it, you are also afraid to have it. Fear is an illusion, a resistance to having what you want. Need, fear, illusion and resistance all begin with lost bonding, but bonding is not so much lost as thrown away in order to gain independence. To get what you want is to step up and shine in your life and this is your greatest fear. All of your defenses are set up to keep this hidden. Your problems are part of this defense. Your chronic issues are especially intent on keeping you away from your purpose and your destiny. Embracing your purpose and destiny gives you a happy life, which progresses on to Heaven on earth, which then progresses on to the realization of Heaven.

Your independence is your desire to do things your way. You don't realize that to do things your way is to not follow the true unfolding of the Tao. So you get off the path. You leave your center. You get into pain and then run further away from your center by trying to dissociate the pain. Your life becomes a muddle. You no longer follow the Holy Spirit's plan for a golden life for yourself. You run from yourself and your greatness/purpose. You resist the Beautiful Life Story that's been waiting for you.

Some of the fears you have are silly, such as: "If I have it all, then I'll die." No, then your ego would die and you will awaken from this dream. You will be transcendently happy.

It is time to be courageous. Melt your fears, both conscious and subconscious, into your need. Such an integration of two negatives will create more wholeness. As soon as you don't need something, you can have all you want. As soon as you're not afraid to not have it and not afraid to have it, you can have all you want. Integration creates this easily. Melt your fears together. Melt them down to pure light and join them together. Then melt your light and your need together, making more light. Any other emotions that come up can be integrated for even more confidence.

Chapter 75

Be First, Do Second

Be first and do second. Your being is your center, your place
of absolute peace. It is your spirit and your light. So many
people waste time in their doing. You do things to make
yourself more secure and so you can have pleasure. But much
of your doing is a defense against feeling valueless and there
is nothing more pleasurable than your being. It brings the
profound peace that brings profound joy. It is the foundation
of love. It is where happiness comes from. It is out of peace
that abundance is born. The more peaceful you are, the
more you realize that every answer you will ever need has
always been within you and that guidance is always present.
Your peace allows you to hear and also to receive inspiration.
It is this quiet mind that restores you physically, mentally and
emotionally. It is this quiet mind that is spiritual, because it is
in this frame of mind you can hear the Voice for God and
receive much more grace. In mastery, you naturally listen.
When direction comes in, you move. Until then, you enjoy
the peace of being. So doing is at a minimum and what you
do becomes effective. This saves so much time and doesn't
wear you out in trivial pursuits.

So, today, choose *being* over doing. Even when you are
called to do, you could let your *being* do it through you. Your
being is rich and effulgent. It radiates light and blesses all
those around you. Grace and miracles are a natural part of
the mind of *being*. The more time you spend enjoying your
being, the more effective you become.

Chapter 76

The Illusion of Independence

Independence is a role and thus it is not freedom. At its best, independence shows resourcefulness and confidence. At its worst, it is dissociated and would rather split or stay apart than have ease, success or partnership. What I am speaking of here is dissociated independence rather than the natural stage of growth you experience after dependence on the way to interdependence.

People leave bonding for independence but it never gives them what they want. They have separated themselves for something that can never fulfill them. Fulfillment is the goal of interdependence, because partnership and mutuality are what you want as they contain more success, abundance, intimacy and creativity. Only radical dependency is beyond interdependence. And radical dependence is in the high reaches of spirituality.

You don't have to look very far to see your mistaken delusion about independence and how you thought it would make you happy. If you could raise your subconscious mind up so that it was conscious, you would see that every trauma you have ever experienced contained the secret desire for independence. Every problem you have also contains your secret desire to remain or become more independent. You break bonding to have this independence, only to find, if you care to observe closely, that it did not make you happy. It's a role and a role does things but doesn't receive. So there's not the enjoyment that you'd hoped for. It has the form and not the feeling of freedom. Not only can independence not receive, it is always in constellation with the roles of the needy-victim and sacrificial-martyr. You don't just take on independence, you also take on the whole family of dependency and sacrifice to go with it.

There is a glamour to independence, especially when you are dependent and feel under the yoke of something or someone. You've had independent heroes and anti-heroes but you have not mastered the *inter*dependent hero.

It's time to integrate into your higher mind all of your constellations of needy-victim, dissociated-independence and sacrificial-martyr personalities. Ask how many of these you have and then choose that it be so. These constellations bring feelings of deadness, being stuck, exhaustion and being caught in a rut. It's time to graduate to interdependence where bonding is restored and partnership is a way of life.

Chapter 77

The Courage to Feel Your Feelings Wins Your Heart Back

The courage to feel your feelings wins your heart back. This is crucial for your ability to partner and for getting over your fear of success and intimacy. You have big emotions stored inside you. Every split in your mind carries fear, guilt and other forms of emotional pain. When a part of your mind, as signaled by a person or event, moves toward you in attack, the pain of the split becomes acute, rushing past denial and dissociation, triggering what's inside and bringing it to the surface. Having the courage to feel your feelings will bring together a part of your mind that was split and a part of your heart that was broken. You can wade through the emotions one after another, feeling them until they are released into a state of peace. Or you can move through them like a bullet to get to the other side. But if you turn away from them and attempt to be defensive, you will keep, and typically increase, the pain inside. You will attack yourself and others. You will deny and defend. You will dissociate and turn your back on the emotion, leading you into the constellations of roles around victim, independence and sacrifice. This prevents you from learning, receiving and growing. This leads you to act in a righteous way, all the while feeling guilt inside. Your courage allows you to accept, forgive, let go, integrate and commit to your next step. This lessens the pain within and makes you happier and healthier.

Any problem or setback contains emotions. Having the courage to pull back every defense and bring the light of your heart and mind to all the buried emotions brings the peace that shows an integration has occurred. Lean into your emotions. Be aggressive with them. They are not the truth and you can have the truth. Want it with all your heart. Your pain, need and illusion all have the same dynamics. They occurred at the same time.

It is difficult when we get hit with something painful or shocking to remember to head straight to the heart of the emotion, where it will give way to another emotion, but you can do it. Every time you go to the heart of an emotion, something more essential shows itself. Do this until you reach profound peace. Set it as your goal and intention, and as soon as something comes up, ask Heaven's help and guidance and dive into it. You can do this until all of the emotion has left you in the peace that creates new beginnings in your life.

Chapter 78

Ill Health is Displacement of Emotions onto the Body

To not experience our emotions fully is to let them build up in the body. Our body is basically neutral. Left without the conflicts of the mind, the body would just go on and on until it was no longer needed. Every emotion shows an expectation, a picture or rule about what should have been. As your rules are broken and your expectations are led to frustration or disappointment, the pain that was inside comes to the surface. This pain was a place that you broke bonding and blamed another for wounding you. This is the past pain that wasn't fully experienced because if it were, then you would have re-bonded. You would also understand that you used the person you blamed as your excuse not to show up or live your purpose and destiny.

One form of healing gets you back in touch with the emotions that you have buried and been taking out on your body. Of course, there is anger in your life because there is both self-attack and attack on others. There is also blame and judgment because they go hand and hand with attack and grievance. But if you felt through those emotions all the way, you would also notice your feelings of guilt and failure. Of course, there is frustration, disappointment, expectation, pushing yourself, holding on and perfectionism covering loss. This sadness, if left to gather in your mind, becomes depression, which lowers your immune system and is a frequent source of illness. There are the heartbreaks that come from old and ancient splits in the mind. For example, adult heartbreaks in relationships are reflective of childhood heartbreaks. Adult heartbreaks are the fruit of the tree while the childhood one was the root. Your most painful defeats and losses are reflective of ancient splits in the mind. When these try to come back to a joining with the part of your mind you identify with, the pain between them comes up. When it does so, if it is stifled under victimization, righteousness, anger or grievances, then it gets displaced onto the body. When the body gets full of these poisons then it leads to illness or accidents.

All the old splits in our mind make us fearful and resistant. Now is the time to be vigilant for the emotions that await us as we go to heal the splits in our mind. The first step is to catch yourself in them instead of reacting, and the second step is to be willing to experience them without projecting them onto a person or situation and making your emotions about someone else. That this person or situation brought these emotions up is actually a gift for your healing. You deny so much but the pain that comes up is what is next on your curriculum of healing. The pain you can still feel or remember from the past is the unlearned lessons and unfelt emotion that want to be felt to completion. Once you are willing to experience the emotion, you can use all of the other healing principles to accelerate your healing. Where there is separation, joining would help. Acceptance would heal where you are stuck. Forgiveness of others and yourself would heal your hidden fear and guilt. Letting go would both open and restore you. Integration would bring new wholeness from a split in your mind where the pain lurked. Commitment moves through the old split, which is causing the fear that keeps you at a standstill. Helping another puts you both back in the flow. Centering returns you to yourself. Grace washes away what blocks you and replaces it with the remembrance of love. But all of these start with the courage to face and feel your emotions while keeping strong your desire for the truth.

Ill health and injury shows a great displacement of emotion. At the deepest level, you are calling for help, yet all of the need, pain and grievances inside you have taken over and now you are vengeful. Naturally, the emotion of vengeance is repressed and denied because it doesn't fit your picture of yourself. The more resistance to vengeance there is, the more that emotion is reinforced, buried and stuck inside you. Otherwise, healing would be no big deal. You'd recognize that it was you who set up the whole thing, take responsibility and you'd pass on to the next step. It would be no big deal. You would acknowledge your part in it, integrate it and peace would be restored.

Chronic illness and bone injury usually speak of unconscious issues, ones that are part of your soul pattern. Soul patterns are what stop you from realizing the love, joy and power of your spirit. You can go through layer after layer of emotion as you feel and heal and it brings more light where there were ancestral and karmic patterns. Yet, if you are suffering from something, it means you came simply to feel it and thus heal it as you return to wholeness and innocence. Or you can forgive yourself the emotion, the situation and the other person involved until you feel free and easy.

So power up and be willing to face the emotions on your plate instead of using your body as the whipping boy of your mind.

Chapter 79

Our Split Mind and Independence Defends Against Emotion

The breaking of bonding in trauma and problems leads to the pain of being a victim, but it also leads to independence and finally sacrifice. These are roles that dissociate you. Every time you see evidence of one of these roles, it shows you a place where your mind is split. The result is you want love and success but you want independence more. Since independence is part of a constellation of roles that includes the painful victim role, you would naturally stop investing in your ego if you fully realized what was going on. To remedy this, the ego brings out two of its best weapons for defense – denial and dissociation. The problem with these defenses is that instead of getting rid of the pain, the ego locks it inside you, thus strengthening itself. This gives it the cache of emotion needed for a negative pattern, and a problem or overreaction later. This type of defense makes you afraid of your emotions, as if they were something special rather than just a natural event that could be used for healing.

Your denial makes you naive and sets you up for a future rude awakening when something 'blindsides' you. It is bad enough that the dissociation blocks receiving and enjoyment, but also your feminine side is disregarded and undervalued. More and more this blocks your heart. Losing your heart to dissociation makes you a 'talking-head', locked into a dissociated intellect, having a hundred good ideas but not knowing the truth. This produces emotional deadness at work, at home and in the bedroom. As with any defense, it pushes to the surface the emotions it was defending against. So need and pain, hurt and heartbreak, and guilt and failure eventually come to the surface, sometimes as a matter of course and other times because of some outside trigger. Until they do come out, there is loss of the ability to feel open-hearted and give yourself 100%.

With your dissociation you lock away gifts and good events along with the pain. A line in *A Course in Miracles* speaks of how we have dissociated Heaven Itself with our dissociation.

Healing is resolving or dissolving the emotion between two parts of our mind, allowing integration. The split mind sets you up for a trauma and every problem you have is the manifestation of your split mind. Trauma comes about because of your desire to hide from your power and greatness, as well as to gain independence and do things your way. This split mind plagues you. You want something and you don't want it. You work hard for something and you resist it at the same time. You want success and you don't want it. You want love and don't want it because when you do actually succeed or have love, you re-bond. The ego resists that because it is the death knell for the ego. Your split mind and the dissociated independence, which is what the ego is made of, are healed in the bonding. So all the healing you do brings your split mind together, making you more whole, healing the pain and dissociation and allowing you to receive.

Chapter 80

Independence Harms You When It is Dissociated

Independence harms you when it is dissociated. Independence is a natural stage of life that everyone goes through. Yet, when it is dissociated it means there is unfinished business from the Dependent Stage, when you were a child and in your first relationships. It means there are important lessons that were not learned at these times. An unlearned lesson means saved-up pain, need, fear, guilt and resistance. It also means that there is heartbreak and rejection you have not gotten over, and as a result either you continue in a heartbreak/victim pattern or break away to do things your way. Both are revenge patterns. It also means that feelings of guilt, failure and unworthiness, mostly stemming from family dynamics, have been relegated to the subconscious. The problems and pain are still inside but now they are covered over. They still affect you; you are just blind to it. You have cut off the pain. You become numb as a result. Now the problem with living under the anesthetic of dissociation is that you only experience a small part of your feelings about the event. This can be dangerous if we don't realize we are injured. It can also cut us off from the realization we need some fire and vitality in our life. Typically, you run away from pain, need or emotion, all of which are projected outside. You especially tend to shoot needs on sight, even when they are connected to those you love. There is the tendency for you to run because you are more connected to your independence and its defenses than you are open to your partner. The more dissociated you are, the more you are righteous about your position. Some people at the deepest levels of independence talk themselves into winning at any cost. If they are deeply dissociated, they can sometimes believe they are above the law and instead bend or use it to their advantage. This feeds the greed that comes from the need, which is covered by the dissociation you used to cover up the pain when you broke bonding to become independent.

Now is the time to begin to remove this dissociation that causes you to lose your heart and do things by rote rather than authentic choice. It blocks your ability to receive, and enjoyment is given up just so you can keep the upper hand of independent control. You are blind to the fact that making everything political, as independence does, robs you of joining, mutuality and equality, all of which would lead you to the next stage of interdependence. You think you have the world on a string but actually you are carrying it on your shoulders. You have blind spots but think you know it all. This leads to problems both at work and in relationships. Having so much dissociated independence leads you into denial, and denial leads to rude awakenings. It is time for you to wake up. Even the most advanced people have pockets of dissociated independence. For the most part, society has not yet advanced beyond dissociated independence where the feminine is not fully valued, receiving is frightening and you have the belief you need to do everything yourself, all the while forgetting partnership and grace.

Chapter 81

Only Our Split Mind Stops Us from Receiving What We Want

Only your split mind stops you from receiving what you want. To want something wholly is to have it. Whatever you want with your whole mind, you create. Your split mind, which comes about whenever you lose bonding, both wants what you want and doesn't want it. At subconscious and unconscious levels, when bonding is lost, it shows that it was your choice because you fell for some ego payoff. This includes hiding, staying small, running from your purpose, trying to protect yourself from a certain fear, attempting to pay off guilt, getting attention, an attempt to get a need met, anger, revenge, control, being right and many more. Every event is meant to be a form of attack both on another and on yourself.

You turn away from having what you want. You make the mistake of having a problem or trauma because you were afraid to step up to a new level of giftedness, which would have saved the day and easily solved the problem before it occurred. You were afraid to shine and hence you are thrown into a learning situation that can be quite painful.

Now, whenever you head toward success or having more intimacy, you face the original crossroads of whether to follow the path of your higher mind or to follow the ego path that has some kind of dark allurement. To choose correctly, to want a better way, to acknowledge your mistakes, to be willing to open the door to your soul's gift and receive Heaven's gift for the situation, to embrace your purpose and destiny, would all restore bonding and create the partnership that spells greater success and intimacy.

Everything that bridges, forgives or integrates naturally brings your split mind together. When you commit to something or someone, it also brings together splits in your mind from the past, generating more confidence, wholeness and innocence. This makes achieving and receiving easy. Know that when there is scarcity or difficulty in achieving anything, there is a split mind. Doing some simple inner work before any action is taken allows you to have what you want much more easily.

Chapter 82

Every Painful Experience is Also Revenge

Every painful experience is also revenge. Lurking deep in the mind there is a hidden part that is wreaking revenge through every painful event that happens to you. As it states in *A Course in Miracles*: "Attack is not discrete." To attack yourself is to attack significant people around you, and a painful event is both attack and self-attack. Naturally, you relegate this to the deepest part of the subconscious mind and the unconscious. You do not suffer alone. You enroll significant others in your suffering.

Working with thousands of people since my early days, I have discovered that some victims were even getting revenge on parents long dead or partners long gone. They were seeking revenge for some old grievance on people who were no longer in their life. They were fighting old battles about something they had not gotten over. There was some need not fulfilled and they were caught in a heartbreak-grievance-revenge pattern that always leads to more heartbreaks, and so the pattern continues.

Hidden under revenge is always guilt because there is a place in your mind where, when you were wounded, you could have stepped up, embraced your soul gift and Heaven's gift, your purpose and your destiny, all of which would have transformed the situation. The person you hold the grievance with would not have been a 'bad guy', you would not have suffered in any way, nor would there have been pain on anyone's part. This, of course, is hidden even deeper than the revenge issue.

Pain need not be. I have found that all pain can be transformed, so it is not the essential truth. It is true that you experience it but it is not the TRUTH. It signals a mistake on your part. You learned the lessons of physical pain as a child: "Don't put your finger in the fire." But you have yet to learn that lesson emotionally. You keep much about your emotions in the subconscious. This means what you let yourself experience is only half the picture.

In the Dependent Stage of your life, you are learning about how to give yourself, how to study and develop mental intelligence. However, as you reach the Independent Level you are learning about *emotional intelligence*, and about your subconscious mind because you have buried so many emotions and patterns from the Dependent Level there. Learning about your emotions and what you buried is helpful for everyone, starting with you. Only when you allow yourself to see what you have been doing that was a mistake, can you begin to realize that you have a choice in the matter and that you can fix it. You can heal your split mind. You can restore your bonding. You can embrace your gifts. You can say a big "Yes" to the next step. A trauma, heartbreak or defeat, is not only an act of revenge, it also begins a revenge pattern. This sets up a life of getting back at others through attack or self-attack. This, and the guilt that goes with it, locks you into a pattern of trauma, defeat and heartbreak, which is deleterious to your happiness and health on many fronts.

Now is the time to become aware that there is much more going on in your victim events than meets the eye. It is not so much what others are doing to you, but what you are doing to yourself through others. Guilt and the need for self-punishment lead to trauma. Fear of the next step and of your gifts and greatness leads to trauma. Power struggles and demands lead to trauma. It is time to become wise to the ego's use of the subconscious. This ego strategy is a way of seemingly getting rid of pain and guilt, while secretly holding on to it to build up the walls of separation. You can change your mind and espouse awareness and healing as your goals. You can deal with what you buried and make more enlightened choices. You can have the courage to embrace your greatness. You have what it takes for emotional maturity and partnership despite what the ego attacks you with.

Chapter 83

Peace is the Goal of Emotional Maturity

Peace is the goal of emotional maturity because with it you have the confidence to relate and succeed. Peace centers you and puts you back in a flow, freeing you from where you were stuck. From peace comes love, happiness and abundance. It puts you in touch with your value and your loveableness. It opens up the quiet mind, which allows you to hear the Voice of God. Peace means that the inner conflict is over and the split mind that had been generating fear and stopping you comes together in wholeness, bringing emotional maturity rather than dissociation and power struggle. Seeking stimulation or something to meet your need is looking outside you to cover over the place of pain where you split your mind. It will eventually fail, leading you to more pain and disappointment. But peace, on the other hand, generates inner stimulation.

In 1984, while doing a workshop in a grand house, I asked to be shown what peace was all about. "I don't get it," I prayed. "What is peace all about? I'm a guy who likes stimulation. Show me what peace is."

It was just before the lunch break and I was starting to peak on peace even as I sent everyone out for a two hour lunch break. When everyone went out the door, I barely made it to the couch because of the ecstatic joy I was feeling. For two hours I lay on the couch so stimulated by peace I could barely move.

I really knew what peace was all about after that. To be in that much peace continuously would be high level mastery or even to be in an awakened state.

Understanding and acceptance bring peace. Forgiveness brings peace. Joining and commitment bring peace. Letting go and integration bring peace. In *A Course in Miracles*, one of the daily lessons is: "The peace of God is my one goal." It is the portal to Heaven and the means by which you know grace is yours. Peace is the only way to have Heaven on earth.

Chapter 84

The Next Step Is Always Better

The next step is always better. All problems represent a fear of the next step. The ego balks at you moving forward because it loses power and at least some of the separation melts away. The next step is always more successful and contains more relatedness. At one level, every problem represents fear and every major problem represents a fear of the next step and sometimes the next stage.

All around the world I've been asked, "What is the next step? What is *my* next step?"

I reply: "Your ego has hidden it from you because it is so good that you would naturally be motivated to step forward." But what I have also found is that the next step is always better. There is more confidence, connection, ability to receive and enjoy, more ease, and, of course, there will be a new challenge at the next stage as part of your soul's evolution. Then you will deal with a new fear of the next step, that is to give up ego control and replace it with surrender and receiving.

To get to the next step takes willingness, as willingness cuts through fear. Taking the step is not marching into the future. It is saying "Yes!" to it. Saying "Yes!" brings the next step to you. When you are open to receive the next step and its success, it comes to you. So commit to the next step. It brings the shift about the easy way. Pray for the next step. Want the next step with all your heart. Manifest for the next step and if it is a big one, realize that the fear the ego has stymied you with is just an illusion. It is the ego that has something to lose, but you are not your ego or your body. You are a timeless spirit. And you have everything to gain by going forward. The next step is always better.

Chapter 85

Heartbreaks are Pieces of Your Own Mind That Want to Come Home

Heartbreaks in the present speak of heartbreaks in the past that haven't been healed. A heartbreak is the fruit of the tree; the roots are buried in the past. Some may even have soul or ancestral roots. When anything that big of a painful nature occurs, it is so that the part that was previously split off in the heartbreak can be re-integrated. At one level, the pain that we experience is old pain as the old, split-off piece surfaces in the present.

One way to heal the split and the pain quickly is to bring the split-off piece back into wholeness. This is a very easy way to heal yourself. The key is to **remember** when you are in that much pain to bring the split-off part of you home. You could do this by imagining that the whole situation was a fracture of your mind, in the same way that every aspect of a dream reflects an aspect of your mind and your self-concepts. Imagine the whole scene melting down to its pure light and power and melting back into you. Then do that with the significant people in the situation. They are self-concepts you have about yourself at subconscious and unconscious levels. See these people as fragments of your mind, melting down to their pure light and power and then once again melting back into you, making you more whole.

Now, imagine the situation as a scene in a play whose act has just ended. The people leave the stage, the scenery is pulled off and the curtain behind is pulled up, revealing the more original scene that led to the present problem. Then melt that scene down to its pure light and power and bring that back to you for wholeness. When there are significant people in the scene, melt these figures in the dream play down to their light and power and bring that light and power into you. Now once again, the curtain behind is lifted and there is another more original scene. Repeat the exercise. Each time you do this it adds another layer of bonding.

You can repeat any level of this exercise until you are in a peaceful place.

Chapter 86

Our Independence is Arrogant

Your independence is arrogant. I'm referring to the dissociated independence in which you have cut off the pain, need, fear and guilt of your earlier dependence. You were dependent to the extent that you were un-bonded, and you were un-bonded to the extent that you wanted to be independent. The secret desire for independence is the desire to go it alone. This is different to the natural desire to grow up, take care of yourself and contribute.

If you viewed the subconscious mind, you would see that every trauma you had was collusion. You could have stepped up and delivered the soul gifts you had received, as well as Heaven's gifts, and obviated the whole painful event. Instead, by refusing to help and by running from your purpose and destiny out of fear of shining you, allowed the negative event to play out. You became the victim of the event, blamed it on another and had your excuse to go independent. Your failure to help, as well as the pain of the victim event and the constellation of independence, victim and sacrifice roles, all added to and attempted to cover up your hardheartedness and your guilt about the event.

It is arrogant to blame another when you could have transformed the whole event. I have taken many thousands of people back to choose correctly and heal the pain and guilt of these old events. It is arrogant to jump into your own life raft from a ship because a negative event occurred that you could have stopped. It is arrogant to leave behind people you could have helped. It is arrogant to blame others for what you did or didn't do. This is exactly what happened but you keep it buried in denial. You use the past for an excuse. You speak of your heroic story, how you made it out alone against all odds, in spite of what others did to you.

Your past is your excuse and anything used as an excuse is arrogant. You use others to maintain the arrogance of your littleness and to allow you to do it your way, when Heaven and your own higher mind have a much better and easier way set out for you. It is arrogant to pretend you did it on your own, without the help of your family or your team, or without Heaven. It is arrogant to struggle, which is used to prove how good you are, when help and grace abound and would heal your ambivalence. It is arrogant to be independent when you are offered interdependence. It is arrogant to blame others when you actually used them as your excuse not to go forward and face your fear and inadequacy. It is arrogant to frame someone by being a victim and denying how much attack you had inside that was expressed as revenge or hurting yourself to get back at another. It is arrogant to ignore the answer that is already inside. It is arrogant to pretend there is not help around. It is arrogant to deny the calls for help and choose independence instead. It is arrogant to 'take' and 'get' rather than receive. It is arrogant to sacrifice and indulge rather than give and receive. Whether you are a man or a woman, if you are stuck in independence you are arrogant to value the feminine so little while exaggerating the masculine. It is arrogant to project and judge, denying your guilt rather than just forgiving yourself and others and learning the lesson. It is arrogant to blame when your blame of others is driven by your guilt. Independence itself is arrogant as it takes no responsibility and all the burden. The extent of your independence is the extent of the victim within you that is a finger of accusation pointing at someone saying: "Look what you did to me."

Both independence and arrogance are unresponsive. You pretend that what's going on around you has nothing to do with you, all the while hiding the subconscious script that led to what happened to you and to those around you.

Chapter 87

When You Are Not Feeling Joy, There is Something for You to Heal

When you are not feeling joy, there is something for you to heal. Joy shows that you are centered and feeling peaceful. It is a sign that you are extending yourself and are open to the beauty around you. Every moment, you are either gladdening yourself or you are making yourself miserable. It is important that you are always choosing the path that is peaceful or leads you to peace. If you choose the path of misery for hidden gains, you will simply have to clear up the defenses and negative emotions later, and they will keep increasing until they get your attention. But if you are committed to healing, you will become even more peaceful because you will be following the path of healing. This builds your success and relationships. It helps you embrace both your purpose and the golden life that is your destiny. Anything else is your ego's plan for you rather than your true plan and Heaven's plan for you.

Here are some major healing principles, one for each day of the week. If you are not joyful, use these principles. Use them often. Even if you are doing well, you can use them to heal unhappy times in the past.

Sunday	Love everything and everyone. Share. Extend yourself energetically.
Monday	All pain and problems are from separation. Imagine your light joining the people or situation that comes to mind. Do this until there is peace.

Tuesday   All pain and problems come from fear. Your willingness cuts through fear. In the face of every problem and upset, say "Yes!" to the next step so the fear disappears.

Wednesday   All pain and problems come from resistance. By giving, you transform your resistance. Give energetically to everyone who comes to mind until you are restored to a happy flow. When you have a problem, **you** could give something that would transform it. Intuit what you could give to transform the situation.

Thursday   All pain and problems come about because of the resistance and pain of a split mind. Accept everything today, even what you don't like, even those you don't like. This allows you to move past where you are stuck. As you accept something, letting go occurs naturally and you are once more in the flow. Accept until you are back in the flow.

Friday   Forgive everyone and everything today to be happy.

Saturday   All upset and problems come from attachment. Find where you are hooked and let go of your attachment, unless you would rather suffer instead.

You can heal yourself and keep learning lesson after lesson. This brings more wholeness and happiness.

Chapter 88

Fear Comes From Judgment

Fear comes from judgment. As you judge, you separate yourself and feel superior to those you have judged. Yet, at an unconscious level, you only ever judge yourself, placing yourself in the vicious circle of superiority-inferiority. As you judge, it increases both your superiority and your inferiority. Placing yourself above someone does not make you feel safe because you feel you always have to defend your 'superiority'.

Judgment is also a form of attack and whenever you do anything to another, you also do it to yourself. Thus the more you judge, the more you feel threatened. You see a world that threatens and attacks because you attack.

Judgment is frightening; it compensates for your guilt but that does not free you because it locks the guilt inside, reinforcing it every time you judge. Your judgment increases fear and pain. There is an astute line from *A Course in Miracles* that states: "From judgment comes all the suffering of the world." You judged when you could have been helping and the splits in your mind that judgment makes also increase your fear. Any split generates fear. Any split generates a conflict. Every conflict generates fear. There is the fear as each side competes and even fights for its own way to get its need met. Judgment is the attempt to get rid of guilt but it exacerbates it, along with the attack on others and self-attack because looking through the eyes of guilt you see no one who is innocent.

Now is the time to commit to giving up judgment. Notice that when you feel upset at someone, think someone is bad or look down on another, you are making yourself unhappy. Recognize that every time you are not feeling good you are judging. Ask Heaven's help and turn every judgment over to be transformed for you. Forgive instead of judge. Help instead of judge. It will make a vast difference in how you feel and in how the world looks at you. Commit every morning and every night to giving up judgment. Examine the day for any time you felt bad; it contains a judgment. Your life could be happy and beneficent instead of fearful and worrisome, if you let Heaven judge for you.

Chapter 89

Your Emotions Show Where You Feel Guilty

Your emotions show where you feel guilty. Any emotion such as anger, hurt or fear makes you feel upset. Any time you feel bad, you feel guilt because that is what guilt is – feeling bad about something. You not only feel the pain or upset of an emotion, you have guilt to go with it. This means the experience of pain that occurs once, continues unless we heal it; guilt locks in the pain as a dark pattern. Guilt is a strong negative reinforcer. So, if you feel bad about something, you reinforce it and get to keep it.

Also, your emotions show you that your mind is split because negativity doesn't come when there is wholeness, but as a result of bonding that has been lost. When emotions come up, they are from past separation being replayed in the present. Here, there is pain and upset. Here, there is guilt. Here, there is stuckness from the past and another avenue to attack ourselves. Yet, here is also a chance to heal the emotions, the situation and the past pattern. Forgiveness is the solvent that dissolves the superglue of guilt; this includes forgiveness of the situation, of ourselves, others and God. Forgive as many times as it takes until peace returns. You do not know whether the situation is coming out of the subconscious or the soul level. So don't think it is not doing any good. Keep choosing to use the healing principle of forgiveness to see everyone's innocence. When you reach that place, you will feel peaceful and happy and you will know the issue is complete.

Chapter 90

Fear Comes From Lost Bonding

Fear comes from lost bonding. When you give up bonding for the blandishments of the ego, you split off from connection with another, with life, with yourself and with Heaven. You become more split-minded and more of a fence-sitter, wanting love and success but wanting independence more. Any split mind produces fear, because all conflicts do. The gap between each part of our mind is held back by the emotions that came about at the time of the split, and one of those significant emotions is fear. The more fear you have, the more paralyzed you become. It is one of the root emotions present in any problem, and it is one of the root emotions you heal as you resolve the problem. Fear shrinks you a couple of sizes smaller. You feel inadequate. You feel that you will lose something significant. You feel separate and that things will not come easily.

You tell stories about how you were wounded and what was done to you. However, buried in your subconscious is the fact that you chose it because you thought you'd have the excuse to be independent and have the gifts your ego offered, such as control and having things your way. These defenses only invited more attacks and unhappiness. You turned away from your strength as a child of God and turned away from the gifts you were being offered, as well as your purpose and destiny. At the root of it all you were afraid to shine. You were afraid of both your greatness and the greatness of your purpose.

The more lost bonding you have, the more you have victim and sacrifice stories, and the more you have hidden or not-so-hidden rebellion going on. Your choice to end the separation, through joining mind to mind or through forgiveness, restores what was lost and gives you back the ease of bonding with its courage and confidence. Bonding and love are synonymous and love heals the illusion of fear that comes from separation. Who could you join with today, where distance has sprung up between you? Do it. It will help everything.

Chapter 91

Fear is Always Illusion

Fear is always illusion. Both fear and illusion spring up when bonding is lost. Your perception of events is colored by all of the splitting away from bonding you have done. A world of separation is a world of darkness and illusion. It comes from all the splits you have made, thinking you'd have independence but instead becoming enslaved by your ego and its needs, righteousness, fear and guilt. Separation generates darkness as you build self-concepts through separation. Once the darkness is in place, the projected self-concepts become the illusions that make the world. All these are based on the ego's fear and guilt that are part of every self-concept.

There is an old acronym in English regarding the word 'fear.'

F -- false
E -- evidence
A -- appearing
R -- real

Fear is a script you wrote at unconscious levels. Nothing can hurt you unless you give it the power to do so. This is a principle of the subconscious and unconscious mind. Whenever you have made a fearful, problematic script, you can change your mind. Fear reflects a need to get something without being able to receive. This is because your need to get something else, in this case independence, is stronger than your desire to receive. The ego is this principle of separation. This is not real liberty but rather a 'do what I want to do' type of thing, regardless of the truth, which is what brings real freedom. Both fear and need feed your illusion. They have you attack, take, seek to get and defend yourself. You then see a world that has something you are trying to get. An old saying is: "When a pickpocket meets a saint, all he sees are his pockets."

Your fear distorts the world. Like worry, it is a form of attack on others and yourself. As you choose trust instead of fear, you correct your perception bit by bit. As you choose forgiveness over fear, the world becomes more benign. As you accept instead of resist, the split in your mind is healed and then there is a new flow and beginning. Fear is a misperception bred by attack and judgment. While you could say that a certain event is frightening or a certain person is dangerous, at one level you are only speaking of yourself and your self-concepts, and the choice to bring these into your life is not by accident. Your ego is attempting more winning, attack and separation. Your higher mind wants to take this opportunity for you to heal this pattern. Your only choice is which part of your mind will you listen to. Your higher mind will give you peace and liberty. Your ego will make things more frightening and cause greater problems.

If something is not working in your life, there is both illusion and fear, fed by some old choice for separation. Let all the people you separated from come to your mind. The separation led to this problem, which is really just your fear of going forward because of some kind of fantasy about something negative occurring. Get your confidence back by joining your light to their light, becoming one light. Do this with memories from the past as well as the present. It is a simple but easy method to heal separation. Do this exercise until you are at peace with each person.

Chapter 92

Nobody Can Hurt You, Unless You Give the Power to Hurt You

Nobody can hurt you, unless you give them the power to do so. When you have displaced your power because you are afraid of it, then you split it off and see a world that seems beyond your control. We have all done this to greater or lesser extent. When you keep getting hit by forces and people outside you, this is evidence of you having displaced your power. At an unconscious level, people and the world reflect your mind. At a subconscious level, what occurs reflects the past. The painful patterns you experience come from old, unfinished business. This began at a place where you broke bonding and refused the opportunity to step up to even greater bonding. This was a refusal of greater power and a throwing away of power under the guise of doing things your way. Yet within you the crossroads at which you made the mistake still exists. If you go back in your imagination to a time before a painful incident occurred, and choose to both keep the power you have and step up to a new level, it can transform the painful situation. As you embrace your power, you can empower others in the situation. Most of the time this completely transforms what occurs next.

Every time you were victimized in any way, any time someone did something to you that you think you didn't want them to do, it shows a place of disempowerment. It is a place where you threw your power away. It is time to revisit all those places and make the choice for power and bonding. Then, as you step up to the new level of power offered and help others in that situation by sharing that power and bonding, everything moves forward. That you are keeping what happened in the past in your mind now, means you are using it as an excuse now. What is that excuse for? And why do you want to prove yourself weak? Your power is your wholeness. It is your innocence. It gives you confidence and, when you have it, you want to share it so everyone has that confidence.

Look around you. Where do you feel hurt and victimized? Go back before the incident happened. Choose again for your power, rather than have it oppose you with obstacles and attack. Then go back to the big incidents of your past and regain your power by making the right choice. Your past is a virtual gold mine of displaced power. It is time to own it back. It will help you and others be happy.

Chapter 93

Fear and Resistance are the Same Mistake

Fear and resistance are the same mistake. They both come about as a result of the illusion that also springs from lost bonding. What you fear you resist, and whatever you resist you make yourself frightened of. Both fear and resistance stop and even paralyze you from going forward. What you have split off in lost bonding you resist and become frightened of. But it is an illusion, no big thing at all, except what the separation and our imagination makes of it. What you are afraid of and what you resist, you misunderstand. Both fear and resistance are built up around loss yet both, by their defensiveness, bring about the loss they are trying to prevent.

Willingness and love cut through fear, and acceptance re-establishes the flow lost by resistance. Both re-bond you and heal the illusion where you have made a mountain out of a molehill. Wherever you are stuck or have resistance of any kind, be willing and accepting today.

Chapter 94

Your Self-Attack Attacks Others

Your attack is not discrete, as A *Course in Miracles* so eloquently states. To attack yourself is to attack everyone, especially those you love. Attack and self-attack go together; you can't have one without the other. To see you suffer is hard on those close to you. Your self-attack is not just a gun that you put to your own head, it is a machine-gun that you take to those around you. Self-attack and attack, which is the other side of the vicious circle, must be given up altogether for there to be safety for everyone. To attack means that you have invested in your ego and believe you are a body. With these beliefs, you will crucify your body and believe God is your enemy.

As it states in A *Course in Miracles*, you never crucify yourself alone. Would the thought of placing the hand of someone you love over your own hand as you hammer in the nail make you pause and reconsider whether you would do such a thing? If you imagined putting the hand of your child, grandchild, beloved or best friend over yours as you were about to attack yourself, would it help you to choose again? If you condemn yourself, it affects more than you alone. In the same way, if you refuse to condemn yourself then it is more than just you who is freed.

The world mirrors your mind. If you realize that the world and its problems are reflecting the hidden aspects of your subconscious and unconscious mind in its self-attack, you could heal by deeper and deeper levels of self-forgiveness. The world will unify as your mind unifies. If you have mercy on yourself, you will have mercy on the world. Letting yourself off the hook blesses the world in more ways than you can imagine. Whenever you see anything negative, you could say, "I won't condemn myself for this" and in this way free both you and what you see, layer by layer.

Chapter 95

Your Busyness is Avoiding Your Power

The Buddha spoke of how busyness was one of the traps that kept a person from happiness. But busyness also serves as a defense in the form of a compensation. It tries to hide and make up for guilt and feelings of failure. It can be a form of sacrifice meant to hide unworthiness, or feelings of inadequacy, or even feelings of being a fraud for having attained the level you have.

Busyness can beget busyness, until you are so burned out you immobilize yourself. Both busyness and burnout are traps of the ego based on the belief you have to 'do it all yourself'.

Any time you move away from your emotions or defend against them, you are moving away from the means to regain your power. As a result, you have pulled back from commitment because you are not available to give yourself fully. As a result, you avoid the power that comes of giving yourself, and you do not include yourself. The emotions and defense are blocking your ability to receive and all of this keeps you feeling old and tired.

A couple of remedies are available. One is forgiveness, beginning with yourself. Next, forgive anyone you feel is not carrying their weight. Next, forgive those from the past that you feel let you down and didn't support you as you felt you needed. At one level, your busyness is an attempt to show them how they should have done it.

Another remedy is to open up the emotions that are denied and dissociated. You can do this only by really wanting to get in touch with these emotions. Then you feel through the myriad of dark feelings until you get to the experience of peace. You can feel these emotions and exaggerate them, knowing that you are moving through them. You are winning back your feminine side so you can begin to receive for all that you do, and enjoy it. You will also be balancing you and your relationship, and moving both into a new level of partnership. This will especially help if you have projected the role of the failure or the shirker onto your partner. This occurs because you haven't given up your competitiveness in which you are trying to prove that you are the very best one.

Another way to move beyond busyness is to give yourself fully to everyone and everything. This level of commitment brings partnership, heals competition, allows you to receive, and creates a flow of success and intimacy once more. Finally, integrating your busyness with the emotions and judgment hidden below it, restores confidence and wholeness.

We live in a busy society in a busy time. It is part of the *zeitgeist*, the spirit of the age. It is a common trap. To move beyond it is to lead the way to partnership and have time enough for love. Commit to that.

Chapter 96

Nobody Hurts Us but Ourselves

Nobody hurts you but yourself. This occurs on a number of levels. First of all, all hurt comes from you resisting and rejecting something. No matter how dire an experience is, if you accept it, then it no longer hurts but is let go of, falling into perspective in your life even integrating into a new peace and confidence. Hurt comes from something you can't accept. Many times it is a form of fighting, a type of emotional blackmail used to control another.

Hurt comes from a pattern; it represents a place where you had already lost bonding. It is the branch of a tree; the roots happened beforehand. While on the surface hurt comes about because someone broke your rules, there is a deeper, more hidden script in which the person or event is exactly following the script that you assigned to them for some mistaken payoff. The question to ask yourself is exactly why you would write this hidden script.

At the level of the subconscious, what has occurred is there for you to learn a lesson. If you learn it, everything is resolved. If not, there is pain to indicate that you made a mistake.

At a soul level, everyone and everything is a projection of your own self-concepts. You only see and experience yourself in the world. To use another metaphor, everyone and everything acts out how you used to be in other 'lifetimes'. At this level, the world is one big mirror.

Forgiveness and integration are called for to bring these errant parts back to wholeness in our mind. What occurs in your life happens by your choice. This is the layer of accountability where you take back your responsibility and your power. Embracing accountability is one of the quickest ways to dissolve big problems. This allows you to give up hurt and grievances, take responsibility and choose more wisely. This removes past grievances and the old guilt that led to these painful situations to pay off the guilt. Once you take responsibility, you can clean up the past and 'bust' yourself quickly when you feel hurt once more. You can use the hurt to find the mistaken pattern and heal it.

Examine all the levels mentioned for hidden payoffs. Let everyone off the hook, including yourself.

Chapter 97

Fear and Need are Two Sides of the Same Coin

Fear and need are two sides of the same coin. When there is fear, there is not wholeness, there is need for something. When there is wholeness, there is no threat, only peace and completion. When there is need, there is the conscious fear it won't be met and there is the subconscious fear it will be met. When you lose bonding, which is when fear and need begin, you also have a split mind. You want love and success, but the side that caused the lost bonding, the side that wanted independence and the control that comes from separation, doesn't want it. Your ego, made of separation, is afraid you will gain love and success, regain the bonding and lose the independence.

Any split in the mind causes conflict, which is one of the main sources of fear. Both fear and need generate resistance in your life and this makes it difficult to make progress. Yet, everything that heals fear or need heals them both at the same time. Understanding and willingness heal fear and need.

- Love heals fear and need.
- Commitment heals fear and need.
- Giving and receiving heals fear and need.
- Forgiveness heals fear and need.

Today, practice understanding, which also heals fear and need. Ask for guidance because true understanding re-bonds you and shows no one is to blame.

Tomorrow, practice willingness. It cuts through fear and moves you beyond need.

The third day, practice love. It melts fear and gives what you think you need, fulfilling it.

The fourth day, practice commitment. It is giving yourself fully and it heals both fear and need.

The fifth day, practice giving. It generates a positive spiral upward with receiving, healing fear and need.

The sixth day, practice receiving. The more you receive, the more you naturally give. Open every door to receive.

And the seventh day, practice forgiveness toward everyone and everything.

This can bring you to even greater peace, healing fear and need.

Each day be aware of need and fear, and what occurs as you practice just a few of the healing principles that heal them.

Chapter 98

Acceptance of Your Emotions Lifts You Up

Acceptance of your emotions lifts you up. You resist and react to most emotions that spring up because they are painful or upsetting. You get angry, hurt or fearful. When you get into that state, it is easy to forget all of your good intentions to use your emotions for healing. So, it is good to set the intention beforehand. If you do this frequently, when emotions do come up, you are ready to respond instead of react to them. To set the intention is simply to choose now, as vividly as you can, to respond effectively in a healing fashion when some upset comes up. This builds your life from the inside out. Past mistakes are corrected. Where you were emotionally arrested, you begin to learn and grow once more. Now, use your will to set your intention and then, when you next feel bad, imagine yourself moving naturally in a healing direction.

Acceptance is one of the core healing principles. A core healing principle can take you all the way to enlightenment. Any type of negative feeling signifies a split in bonding. These feelings are wedged between the splits in your mind that occurred with the lost bonding. They keep you emotionally arrested. To deal effectively with them is to have the integration of these splits occur once more and bonding re-established. To clear out the emotions is simply to accept them rather than resist them. Though you are feeling them, imagine that the emotions are just outside you. As painful as they might be, welcome them into you. When resistance ends, so does the pain. As you bring the emotions into you, see and feel them lifting up your consciousness. If they are super big emotions, you might have your angel or Jesus or Buddha stand next to you, holding your hand. Emotions can also be helpful at weeding out dark influences. So, welcome both the event and the emotions in and let them lift you. As they come in, they bring power back and that is what lifts you. As they come in, they restore your heart and lift up your awareness. Every emotion signals a split in your mind that could be healed with full acceptance of the emotions and the event that gave rise to them. Full acceptance leads to integration. This creates peace, confidence and greater wholeness. It brings back greater balance and more of your heart.

Chapter 99

The Goal is Peace

The goal is peace, but our age is an age of stimulation. All manner of entertainment is available. This can easily reinforce the major mistake in life that something or someone outside you is the source of your happiness. It's not that things and people can't make you happy. It's just that they are not the source of your happiness. Your happiness comes from you; it is within you as your Source. Jesus said it when He stated the Kingdom of Heaven is within.

The gateway to Heaven is through your mind to your spirit, and that is where Oneness is. That is where you are whole and holy. Most of you live on the surface of your lives in the endless movie the outside world provides, projected from your own self-concepts. Yet, it is peace that is the gateway to your spirit. *A Course in Miracles* states how it is in the quiet mind that you can hear the Voice of God. It also says that you hear the Voice to the extent you are willing to hear it.

There is a lesson in *A Course in Miracles* that states, "The Peace of God is my one goal" because in that goal is every other goal that would make us happy. Peace heals the mind. It energizes and restores us. It heals the conflicts that lead to illnesses and injuries. The peaceful mind is the mind of mastery in which one choice could save ten to fifteen years of hard work. The extent of your peace is the extent of your wholeness, innocence and joy. There is no reason necessarily to do anything for it because it comes from your *being*.

Chapter 100

Not Getting Enough Love Comes from Guilt about Having Been Loveless

Not getting enough love from your partner, family or everyone in general comes from guilt about having been loveless. These self-concepts are still inside and we punish ourselves for them.

Over the years, I have worked with many people who feel that they aren't getting enough love. I have traced this back to times, usually in childhood, when they felt that they were heartless and were not giving love. This incident is usually forgotten but it has such a major impact on people's lives. Most of the time these incidents are covered over by victim events where we disguised that we were hardhearted and could have saved the situation, rather than used it to separate. Our lack of love back there generated a self-defeating pattern, also known as karma, and it comes as a result of guilt. Many times the incident you feel guilty about was a very minor one. Yet, the love that is missing is a big issue in your life now. Once you return to the place where you felt you were heartless and reverse your response, it has the effect of changing your life in the present in a really beautiful way.

Almost everyone can use more love and, of course, Heaven is giving more than you can ever receive but your guilt shuts down the channel of receiving from Heaven and from those around you.

Ask yourself:

If I were to know when I closed down the channel to receiving love, it was probably at the age of...

If I were to know who it was I acted lovelessly toward, it was probably...

You may even have a story about how this person victimized you, but if you had not acted in a loveless way toward them, they would not have had the love that healed the need/pain that had them act so badly. Whatever the case, go back to that scene, ask that you and this person be returned to as many centers, always higher and deeper, that would free you both and have you act in a loving, responsive way toward them. Carry this peaceful, centered, loving feeling from that incident all the way up through your life. Notice the difference as the story of your life is rewritten with love and how the present time changes so that you are responded to in a loving way. If the results are not all that you wished for, it is because there is at least one more situation to heal in order to remedy your feeling of not receiving enough love.

Summary

Your maturity is up to you. If you do not learn about your emotions, it is easy to become a bully, a cry-baby or a martyr. As a bully, you have lost your heart and it's easy to do to others what you wouldn't want done to you. Yet, because you have dissociated, you are either blind or don't care. You will mistake domination and control for power. If you have become a cry-baby, you will attract victim events to you like a magnet. You will be weak and powerless and take no responsibility for your situation. Or, as a martyr, you will live a life of sacrifice with its secret competition and attack, resentful of the sacrifice and wanting others to be in sacrifice to the same degree as you. In your fusion and co-dependency you will shoulder everything, and you will disempower both others and yourself by stepping in to do it for them when you could have had faith in them and the situation. Martyrdom and sacrifice attempt to reaffirm your value in a way that doesn't work in the long run and puts you above others in the short run.

On the other hand, with emotional maturity you live a life of partnership and ease. You are honest with yourself, and as a result you have many fewer victim situations, if any at all. You have relinquished comparison and competition. You have stepped off the merry-go-rounds of domination-submission and superiority-inferiority. You have peace instead of the Great Wars of Good and Evil, and the even more primordial war of Right and Wrong that keeps you in guilt. The more emotionally mature you are, the less likely you are to have hurt, heartbreak or revenge. Failure, and its projection of guilt, becomes a thing of the past.

With emotional maturity, you take responsibility for your life and your emotions. You give up blaming others for your emotions when you stop judging and condemning others and, as a result, your suffering is healed with emotional maturity. You gain more and more confidence and play a bigger and bigger game. You bless and make better every situation you come into. You are part of the solution rather than part of the problem. You are no longer afraid of your power and so are more and more adept at leading, being creative, giving love, sharing yourself sexually and dealing with money. Because you include, you are included. Because you show mercy, life is merciful to you. Because you love, you are beloved. Because you give, you get to receive. Because you forgive, you realize that you are innocent. Because you help, help is always available to you. The more you re-bond, the more you open to others and to Heaven, not as a religious belief but as a spiritual experience. You realize that from your twenties onward life is about dissolving your ego, so there is less of you and more of Heaven.

At each step, your awareness and ability to reach out grows. Integrity and the peace it brings become your main goals because they lead to wholeness and happiness. It is the path to Heaven on earth.

All of this occurs through emotional maturity. We use emotions as they were meant to be used, as indicators of what we need to heal and not where others have wronged us. Emotional maturity unifies our mind from the myriad of personalities all wanting their own way. The unity that comes brings unity in our world. Let us take up the courage of the feminine and move beyond competition to real teamwork and living with our whole heart. If we do, we will be blessed with beauty, harmony, health and happiness!

We are constantly being asked to 'man-up', 'soldier-up' or 'cowboy-up', but the real way forward is to embrace our feminine side, which is all about getting our heart back and turning emotions into positive feelings. This will balance society and bring right relationships, instead of the conflicts and deadness now rampant. When we reach interdependence, the world and our lives categorically shift, increasing everyone's love and success. Happiness will become a way of life, augmented by helping others and healing ourselves.